Report for Duty

Report for Duty

Memoirs & Photos of a World War II Veteran

Forrest A. Thornton

iUniverse

REPORT FOR DUTY
MEMOIRS & PHOTOS OF A WORLD WAR II VETERAN

THE HOLY BIBLE, NEW INTERNATIONAL VERSION®, NIV® Copyright © 1973, 1978, 1984, 2011 by Biblica, Inc.® Used by permission. All rights reserved worldwide.

iUniverse books may be ordered through booksellers or by contacting:

iUniverse
1663 Liberty Drive
Bloomington, IN 47403
www.iuniverse.com
1-800-Authors (1-800-288-4677)

ISBN: 978-1-5320-0405-6 (sc)
ISBN: 978-1-5320-0406-3 (e)

Library of Congress Control Number: 2016913596

Print information available on the last page.

iUniverse rev. date: 08/29/2016

Dedicated to

My lovely bride of over 70+ years,
Geraldine Sutherland Thornton

CONTENTS

PREFACE

Over the years I have lived since World War II, I have made many small photo booklets, notebooks with thoughts of events that happened, and have given presentations of my life during the war. But with today's advances in information technology there is almost limitless data available for use.

Many times throughout my tour of duty in the US Army, I was frightened by dangers I faced, mainly during the Battle of the Bulge. There were sounds of artillery fire, bombs and other disturbances but the Lord was gracious and spared me through it all. Now this is what God says in His Holy Word, The Bible: "For the Lord watches over the way of the righteous" (Psalm 1:6a, NIV); "Surely, Lord, you bless the righteous; you surround them with your favor as with a shield" (Psalm 5:12, NIV); "You are my hiding place; you will protect me from trouble and surround me with songs of deliverance" (Psalm 32:7, NIV).

As I began preparing my story of World War II for publication, I realized that I needed to do some research and explain several things that happened along the way. Thankfully, I usually carried a camera in the inside pocket of my uniform so was able to take several hundred photos. Some of the better ones are included in this book and are used to illustrate each story. With the 4 years in service I would estimate that I have over 350 good photos from which to choose.

I realize that many of my cousins and friends were also in this same war. For some reason or another, I never took the time to talk with them about their experiences during this dreadful ordeal. I certainly was not the only one feeling the horrors of war.

My Honorable Discharge shows I was with the 920th Ordnance Company, but it does not show the majority of years during the war that was with the 107th Ordnance Company.

After basic training was completed I was sent to Camp Livingston, Louisiana, to join with the 107th Ordnance Medium Maintenance Company which was engaged in maneuvers there. I stayed with them until March 21, 1945, a period of three years and three months.

Shortly after my return from a furlough that I spent in England in 1945, I was reassigned to the 920th Ordnance Replacement Company at Metz, France. This was the last company to which I was assigned; therefore it is the one that is shown on my discharge records.

Not too long ago at the Bayland Community Center here in Houston, Texas, I was asked to present some of the photos and stories to many who were interested. This turned out quite successfully and several seniors asked if I had published anything. With these thoughts in mind, I purposed to tackle this major project, which I personally found to be pleasingly stimulating to me, and also hopefully to others.

At my age of ninety-six, time is running out very quickly. So, hopefully with assistance from my family as critics, it is becoming even more exciting for me to get this project completed for publication. I do regret thinking of the many men of my ordnance company who are no longer living that could have helped me remember some events. But here, to the best of my memory, is my story.

Forrest A. Thornton
March 24, 2016

ACKNOWLEDGEMENTS

I wish to thank those who helped me throughout the process of this project:

Lois Thornton Hauck -- Thanks for your hours spent proof reading, and the many suggestions for improving the text language and style.

Gary Hauck -- Thanks for your advice and also the preparation of the text for the editors. I am truly grateful for the countless hours you spent on this project!

Jared Hauck and Tim Thornton -- Thanks for your help with the photos. The book would be incomplete without the pictures to illustrate my years in service. Jared, you were patient with me when I kept telling you, "That's the last batch of pictures to work on!"

And thanks to my fellow soldiers and family members who willingly took my picture along the way.

Photos identified by "FT" were taken by the author.

The photos of the author in the epilogue and on the back cover were used with permission, Copyright 2016, Tim Thornton, photographer.

All scripture quotations are given in the New International Version of the Holy Bible produced by the International Bible Society, now known as Biblica, Inc. (1973, 1978, 1984, 2011). While this version was obviously not available during the time of World War II, it has been selected for use here for the ease and benefit of today's reader.

Alvin, Virginia and Forrest Thornton, 1920 - St. Albans, WV

CHAPTER 1

Growing Up in West Virginia

As I peered from my window on the crowded train and waved one last goodbye to my loved ones standing on the train platform, my heart was about to break, especially not knowing if I'd ever see them again. They strained to get a good look at me and I did the same in my small crowded seat while I was filled with many conflicting emotions. The train slowly pulled out of the station as we departed to the first of many unfamiliar and uncertain places.

St. Albans was a tiny, charming town nestled in the hills of West Virginia. The population was so small that most people knew each other, and the ones that didn't soon would because of the friendliness of their neighbors.

Winters were cold and brutal, summers hot and humid. Spring and fall were gorgeous with the colors from seasonal changes making the scenery breathtaking. But the main reason St. Albans was a good place to live was the tight-knit community where most people took care of their own.

I grew up in this town, the oldest of six children. Being the only boy, one would think I had to pamper all of my sisters, especially with them being younger. But as my youngest sister, Nancy, has constantly reminded me over the years, they catered to me. Somehow I never realized the special treatment I received from Mom and Dad when they always let me sit up front with them in their car while driving to church. It never dawned on me that none of my sisters ever got that privilege.

Mom was such a kind and gentle person. Our growing up years were filled with her tender and loving care. She always seemed to have a smile on her face and that gave us such peace knowing that if she could be happy, we could be happy. She took up sewing since she was a talented seamstress and managed to also find time to sew dresses for my five sisters.

We weren't as close to our dad as we were to our mom but respected him for his unselfishness. He taught us by example to be honest in everything and to work hard. Being a storekeeper, he had to be gone most of our waking hours but we knew that he was providing for our family in the best way he could.

I was told that before I could walk, I crawled out of bed and got stuck under my mother's bed as she had taken sick and couldn't get up to tend to me. I kept trying to raise my head but each time it bumped the bottom of the bed. Someone must have pulled me out because . . . here I am!

My Only Spanking

Yes, I guess I'll admit I did have one spanking in my whole life! The doctor had been called for my mother as she was again sick in bed. He brought along some medicinal powder but placed it on the top shelf while he was tending to her. In my boyish curiosity I climbed up there when no one was paying attention, spilled out the contents and made some roads for my tiny car. Dad wasn't too happy with me when he discovered what I had done. I made sure I yelled hard so he'd stop whipping me!

Boyhood Home

Etched in my memory is the one place I will always think of as "home." At the age of three my Dad bought an old, two-story, white-framed house from a man by the name of Wheeler on December 6, 1923. The house was situated at the base of a hill and faced the curve in the busy highway, US Route 60, earlier called the James River and Kanawha Turnpike. This structure was on the south side of the road about one tenth of a mile west of the Coal River bridge and right next door to Dad's general store. It was probably good we didn't have a sidewalk in front of our house because several times cars going too fast left the road or had a wheel come off into our yard rolling into Dad's general store. These events made life interesting.

The house was a backward "L" in shape. Upon entering the front door, I would find myself facing a long hallway and at the end was a door leading onto the back porch. My parents used the bedroom to the left just inside the front door. And to the right was a door into the living area. In back of this room and parallel to the back porch was the dining room with the kitchen beyond. Being the great cook she was, Mom provided us with delicious home cooked meals. A small room in the back corner to the left of the kitchen was a pantry and wash room.

The ceilings of this house were very high, maybe around ten feet. For a little boy such as myself, they seemed enormous. The upstairs was configured similarly to the downstairs but was used mostly as bedrooms. We needed lots of those since there were eight in our family. Over the front porch was a small room that ended up being my favorite playroom, having windows on all three sides. I spent many hours there, playing with my toys. My room was also upstairs but in the northeast corner where I had a good view of the store and the road leading across the bridge into St. Albans. I was able to entertain myself watching the cars go by.

The house was heated with natural gas stoves in most of the rooms. These stoves had an open front with clay radiants in the back that glowed red-hot when lit but did little to actually heat these spacious rooms. We could stand in front of one and be warm on the side facing these stoves but cold on our other side.

We had very poor lighting with each room having only a single gas mantle that hung from the ceiling. In the late 1920s electricity was brought to us but the light fixtures were so crude it hardly made a difference. During this time water lines were installed in our area. This prompted Dad to convert an upstairs storage room into a bathroom. Having five sisters, this was pure luxury even though we still had to go outside and across the back porch to get to this area. We also were thinking we would rather do this than traipse up the hillside to the small and drafty outhouse.

Before the lines were installed, we had to take our baths in a washtub in the kitchen after Mom heated the water on the stove. Saturday night was bath night and carrying the water in a bucket from the well out in the side yard wasn't pleasant, especially during the cold winters. Sometimes the bucket of water left in the kitchen overnight for cooking the next morning had to be thawed out on the stove before Mom could fix our breakfast.

Shortly after my youngest sister, Nancy, was born, Dad decided it was time to tear down the old house and build one that was more comfortable and with more bedrooms (1933). He hired a contractor by the name of Dasher Bowles to build it. This was such a nice house and was so much warmer in the winter than the old one. Some of the lumber from the old house was as good as what could be bought new so they used the older lumber in the framework with some of the 2x4's being about twenty feet long. Dad kept this house until June 16, 1949, when he sold it to a cousin, Dana Loftis. While this new house was being built, we rented one behind Dad's store on Strawberry Road. Mom taught me how to paint so I enjoyed helping her spruce up the walls and ceilings. A hired painter did the outside and soon it began taking shape.

Scarlet Fever

When I was about four years old I had scarlet fever. That's one of my earliest memories, probably because I had to stay in bed for such a lengthy period of time. To entertain me, my parents bought me a toy monkey made of metal. They attached it to the bedpost with a string and when this string was pulled the monkey climbed to the top then fell back when the string was released. It also made a funny, little noise as it went up and down the string.

Cousins by the Dozens

Living next door to my grandparents allowed me to have many good times playing with cousins as they often came for a visit. There were thirty-two cousins on the Thornton side and twenty-eight cousins on the Bird (my Mother's) side. They usually came on a Saturday or Sunday and we got to play all over the hillside in the back of our house. We made roads for my scooter and wagon and also played with a small hoop about eight or ten inches in diameter. This hoop got rolled on the ground with a stick propelling it along. We also liked to play with marbles.

I learned to make things out of wood from boxes from my Dad's store. I not only made a model Viking ship and a Spanish Galleon but I also made little life-sized birds and painted them to look like cardinals, blue jays, etc. I used hay-bailing wire for legs and stuck them in the ground in our front lawn with a sign saying "five cents each." People who passed by bought them which helped me buy my first camera that summer—a folding Kodak 127.

Christmas Joys

Thinking back to my early memories of Christmas in the 1920s, the first things that popped into my mind was the oranges, nuts, and hard candies that we each received in a small sack. In later years, a few chocolate crèmes were added and toys were made from wood or tin. The love and warmth from my tight family generated genuine excitement. Christmases were simple, but very delightful. We always had a live, freshly cut pine tree with unelaborate trimmings. We were told that Santa Claus was the one who brought our toys but it wasn't until I was about nine or ten that someone from school told me there wasn't a Santa. I didn't repeat this for fear I wouldn't get any more toys. One special Christmas, I got an American Flyer, an electric train popular since the early 1900s. On another Christmas, I received an erector set. The year I got a nice sled, wouldn't you know it only snowed once!

Summer Vacations

Nearly every summer we went somewhere as a family for a week of vacation. I'll never forget the summer in 1932 when we went to Virginia Beach and took my grandfather, Baxter Bird. It was his first time to be back in the state where he was born. At age seventy-six, he had never seen the ocean before. I can still visualize him standing with one foot on a park bench and his chin resting in his hand, just taking it all in.

In 1934 we went to the Chicago World's Fair, called "A Century of Progress." In August 1937 we went to Washington, DC, and were able to visit many of the historic buildings. We even got to tour the White House but Franklin D. Roosevelt wasn't in that day.

It was an all-day trip to drive to Huntington, which was only a forty-mile trip from St. Albans. We loved going there because there was an amusement place called Camden Park. A good bit of the narrow road paved with brick had a curb on each side. It seemed that every few years they were widening this road to accommodate the cars as they got larger and increased in number. Also many of the dangerous curves were taken out. Roads in the early days were usually put on land that had no other use. They followed the creeks where unpaved roads sometimes were put inside the creek beds.

Many summer trips were made out to the country to either Dad's home-place or Mom's place of birth. One day, when I was six, we made such a trip but our car came to a sudden stop in the middle of the dirt road. It was making a loud siren-like noise. We had run over a large rock that had smashed the oil pan. Fortunately, we were within walking distance of the Thornton home-place. Dad somehow got the pan cover off and pounded out the dent, repairing it enough to get us home. Thankfully, we didn't have to walk the eight miles back on those unpaved roads. We were also glad that the rain held up because when the red clay got wet, our car could have gotten stuck.

First Radio

Dad was among the first few people in St. Albans to have his own radio. I remember the first one being a large, table model with three huge dials. All three dials had to be set at just the right place to get a station signal. Even then the sounds coming were mixed up with the noisy static and squealing sounds.

We were able to get stations as far away as Chicago - WLS, Cincinnati – WLW, Pittsburgh – KDKA, and Nashville – WSN. A car battery located in the basement powered our first radios. Among the big events that caused neighbors from all around to gather at our house were the prizefights. One evening they came to hear the champion prizefighter, Jack Dempsey.

Horseless Carriage

Dad's first car was a used 1915 Model "T" Ford that he bought in 1920. He told me he bought it from a man who just came into the store one day and wanted to sell it. After Dad's cousin, Dana Loftis, showed him how to start and stop it, he got in and drove three miles to Carter's garage at the junction of old state route 17, now US 35 west of St. Albans. When he got there he didn't know how to back up to turn around so he ran it up an embankment and let it coast back down. In the meantime, he had at least three flat tires before he got back home. What an adventure! I guess the tires were pretty flimsy back then. Some of the other cars he had over the years were: Willis Overland, Nash, Graham Page, Dodge, Plymouth, Hudson, and Rambler.

I remember one of Grandpa's (W.P. Thornton) cars. It was a Franklin with an air-cooled motor. It had a sloping windshield and an outside sun visor. Over the years our family became so large we had to get a bigger car called a "seven-passenger." It had two small folding seats between the front and back seats. We used to fuss about who would get to ride in them but as I mentioned before, usually my parents let me get first choice. Grin. Going for a car ride in those days was much slower but also much more enjoyable since we passed houses with people waving to us from their front porches as we went by. Even those we didn't know waved.

School Days

My first year in school, 1926, was at Fairview Elementary, one mile west of the Coal River bridge in St. Albans. The old, two-story frame building was bursting at its seams. I can remember Mrs. Ida Bryan being my first grade teacher and Mr. B.Y. McCormick, the school principal. Unlike schools today we started out each morning with the pledge of allegiance to the flag along with prayer before classes began. Sometimes we even recited Bible verses. Every once in a while, some of the kids who thought they were clever recited the shortest verse, "Jesus wept." In 1927 we moved into a new building where I continued to attend through the seventh grade.

One boy in my fifth grade class wanted to buy an ice cream cone at the stand just across from the school. When he asked for a cone, the clerk said, "I can't sell it to you. I have only enough ice cream for one more cone and if I sell it to you I won't have any for the next customer."

One of my most enjoyable classes was penmanship. We had scriptwriting with a pen that you dipped in ink. I received a nice certificate after completing this class. Sixth grade was memorable because a classmate, the class bully and son of my first-grade teacher, jumped me and started pounding, even tearing my shirt. He ended up getting a good whipping from the principal, Mr. Guice. The bully later told me that he thought I was trying to steal one of his girlfriends. Imagine that!

Because of overcrowding in eighth grade, eight of us were transferred to a different school, Central School in St. Albans. This started out to be a difficult transition for me but later became a good one since I met two brothers who ended up being lasting friends, Delmer and Charles Turley. Charles later was best man in our wedding and eventually would become my brother-in-law.

That year we had an operetta and also a black-face, white-gloved minstrel show. We had an excellent music instructor, Mr. H.C. Pittenger. Under his direction I participated in several operettas and also sang tenor in the choir at First Baptist Church, where he was the choir director. I joined the high school band one year and carried the school colors. The band that year got to go to Huntington to participate in the state high school band festival.

One of the stores in St. Albans was called Hines' Hardware. I always liked to go there because Gordon Hines, the son of the owner, let me help in the store. Gordon had his own dark room in the basement of the store and taught me how to develop film and make prints with enlargements. I loved it so much I made my own dark room at our home on West Main Street. This carried over into the latter part of my life where I continued to enjoy photography. We had a camera club in school that included contests on special subjects. I didn't win anything, but I learned much and it was a lot of fun.

During the summer I visited Delmer and Charles so that we could sneak off and swim in Coal River. This river was across a field in back of their house. Although it was very deep at this point and quite dangerous, we still ventured out but not too far. I'm sure it wasn't the safest place to swim but we did it anyway. I know I wouldn't want to do it now.

Learning to Drive

Dad let me practice learning how to shift gears on his car by letting me drive back and forth in our driveway and the parking lot beside of the store. But before I could do this, I first had to wash the car. I suppose the car was kept pretty clean in those days since I wanted to practice driving.

I was about sixteen when one day, upon returning home from the state fair at Institute, West Virginia, just across the river, Dad let me get behind the wheel on the road home even though it was narrow with quite a bit of traffic. We somehow made it all the way in one piece. Later my uncle, Lewis Bird, my Mom's brother, took me in his car to Kanawha City. The state police building was inside a large fenced-in area with the narrow entrance having two large brick posts. If you could get by these without any damage you could probably drive okay. The trooper went with me for my driving test, and thankfully I did get my license and kept driving until 1998!

Music Lessons

My parents loved music, so they gave each of us the opportunity to take some music lessons. In his early years, Dad had attended a "singing school," as they called it. A traveling tutor conducted this school for short periods at one of the country churches or schools. This instructor taught the different sounds that the notes represented. They were shaped notes with each shape having a different tone, also called the Do, Re, Mi, etc. scale. It was begun in 1801 to help singers find pitches within the scales.

One day I found out that a music store in Charleston was offering music instruction with the purchase of an accordion. I bought a small twelve-bass which I soon outgrew. I had to ride the interurban trolley, called a streetcar in order to have my lessons at the Galperin Music Company. The ride was quite an experience, especially where it crossed the Kanawha River at Charleston. The trolley shared the railroad bridge, which was an open-steel, framed structure, and crossing this bridge when you looked down all you could see was water. At Christmas, to my delight, Dad bought me a one-hundred-and-twenty-bass Hohner, which was a better sized accordion for me. The music store sponsored an accordion and saxophone band and in September 1939, we gave a concert.

Family Store

Compared to others, our family not only survived but also did very well during the depression days. Dad was a merchant in St. Albans, so we didn't have to struggle as some did. We didn't have everything we wanted but, thank the Lord, we did have most of the things we needed.

My grandfather, William, or Billy as he was called, owned a store that was built around the time of his marriage in 1890. His brother, Thomas Jefferson Thornton, also had his own store but his was in Lincoln County. Therefore, the merchandising business was in the family. Grandpa's store was a one-story, wooden-frame building in Putnam County with a high, front panel and a side room that was for warehousing. There was a loading platform in the front and they sold everything the farmers needed. Dad worked in his father's store and seemed to develop a good sense of managing.

My parents moved to St. Albans after they were married and rented a building that had been a stable as a place to set up housekeeping. Dad said they had to do a lot of work to make it livable including throwing out the manger! He also rented a store building from his uncle and this was the beginning of over forty years of being a merchant.

At first, at this new location, he saw that people walked by his store every day but didn't once venture inside. One day he put up a sign saying "UNDER NEW MANAGEMENT." That must have helped because people started coming in regularly and business started booming. Much of the trade came from people working at the Bowman Lumber Company. Also with the ferry running from Coal River Bridge to Nitro, more people streamed in. As business improved, their lifestyle improved so they moved into a house just next to the store.

Around 1919 a fire destroyed the store and several houses, including my parents' home. My parents were in shock for quite a while, but thankfully no one was hurt. After hearing about the fire, Grandpa Thornton came to town to offer some much needed assistance. This prompted him to buy some property, including a store building next to our house and this was the beginning of a partnership called, "Thornton & Son."

There were several other fires, one being caused by a vagrant who caught the back door on fire as he was trying to break in. The second time was about ten-to-fifteen years later around Christmas 1926 when I was six years old. The fire started in a building next to the store and sparks caught our family store on fire along with the building across the street. They had a time trying to find out what started this fire which came to within five feet of our house. Dad was able to grab the things from the safe in the store and move our necessities out of our house in time. The store burned to the ground but the fire department was able to save our house. My sister Jean and I were sent to our grandparents' house until the damage to the house was repaired. We found out later that the fire had been started by a man who had fallen asleep after drinking and smoking in bed.

The next day I went with my Uncle Roscoe to look at the damage. After poking around in the ashes we found some coconuts that had been roasted in the fire. We cracked one open and ate it. To this day I love the taste of coconut and I'm reminded of that time in my life whenever I eat some.

A new store was built but this time it was a two story red brick and tile building. While the store was being built, an empty building across the street was rented temporarily until the new store was finished in 1927. This store was still a typical country-style store, filled with the aromas of fresh ground coffee. The ceiling was made of embossed tin with a beautiful design. The back storage room even had a manually-operated elevator. In this same room was a large floor scale that was used to weigh out bulk quantities of grain and other items. Dad often would proudly take me back there and have me get on it. He then would grin and say that I was getting big like him. The upstairs was used mainly for display of large items like furniture, carpeting, wallpaper and paint. Kerosene was sold in bulk and was used for lanterns. It came in a large drum with a pump that measured out into quart containers that the customers brought in with them.

I don't know if Dad was aware of this or not but when I was young, probably seven or eight, I used to sneak to the back corner where the surplus candy was stored. Ordinarily it would be in the display cases directly in the front part of the store. But much of the candy didn't fit so it was moved here. I sneaked some chocolate creams from a round tin and let each one melt slowly in my mouth, not chewing lest I be discovered.

While I was still young, my Dad let me help restock the shelves. Later on he let me help fill the orders of some customers especially if they were relatives. I had to weigh out the sacks of any of the bulk items like dried beans or potatoes. I also sliced and weighed bacon and lunchmeat. Each item had to be written on a charge pad and priced. In those days there wasn't any self-service. The customers were not to go behind the counter and help themselves but had to wait their turn for a clerk to fill their order. Many items were inconveniently placed on shelves that were too high for anyone to reach. Some items even had to be reached by climbing a ladder. The store had a long pole with a hook on the end that was used to fish some merchandise from the top shelf, including shoes of all styles and sizes. Various bolts of material could be found on a table near the front. Toys usually came unassembled but it was fun to help put them together.

Mom rarely, if ever, got to shop for her own food supplies because Dad brought home whatever she would need to prepare the mouthwatering meals we had each day. Perhaps she wouldn't have had time anyway, caring for her large family.

Almost everyone used the credit plan and paid their bill on payday. This occurred more during the depression days. Some customers ran up a large account but when they got paid they went somewhere else to buy what they needed. Some never did pay up even after having to be sued for what they owed! Most businesses were having difficulties staying alive during the Great Depression. Dad heard about a plan that became available for merchants and small businesses worldwide to enable them to join into a system that offered special pricing called "Quality Service." Sources of food and other necessities to keep alive were offered at a decent fee. Along with it was the supply of pricing sheets for advertising.

I was still in school but on Fridays after getting home, I joined my Uncle Roscoe, Dad's brother, and we both helped in the store. Uncle Roscoe was just like a big brother to me since we weren't that far apart in age. We even combed our hair alike, with me imitating most of the things he did. Dad told us one day to take the price sheets and stamp them with the store name. After that was completed we walked all over the neighborhood distributing these handbills displaying our Friday and Saturday specials in order to gain new customers.

Paper Boy

During this time I found out our newspaper boy was quitting so I put in for his job and began delivering newspapers with the *Charleston Gazette*. I had thirty-plus customers who paid twenty cents each week. The hardest part about the job was getting up before dawn especially when we had those typical harsh winters. The papers were heavy but I had a large cloth bag to carry them over my shoulder.

Early one morning I was sure I had heard my alarm clock. It was an old wind-up alarm that would make a certain click just before it would go off. I didn't want to disturb the whole house so quickly turned it off. I groggily got out of bed, got dressed and began getting ready to go do my route then remembered I needed to reset the alarm to the time that Mom and Dad needed to get up. To my astonishment, I saw it was only two *am*! Needless to say, it didn't take me any time to undress and crawl back into my warm bed. But of course the real alarm went off way too soon after that. This time I had a more difficult time getting awake. That year I acquired enough new subscribers to the paper to win a free trip to summer camp for a week at Lake Shawnee just north of Princeton, West Virginia. While at this camp I learned to swim.

Jobs

I had several jobs after high school, including working in a drug store where I made sodas and ice cream floats for customers. An older man trained me before he left for another job. The druggist received bulk ingredients for making ice cream along with a package containing different flavors to mix in. The ice cream mixture was put into containers then placed into a freezer contraption. After freezing it was put aside to stabilize before dishing out. Even though the pay was minimal, getting all the ice cream, sodas and fudge I wanted made up for it. I didn't even mind mopping the floor late at night before closing. Soon after that I began working in the bank as a teller and later my sister Jean came to work there, too.

Courtship

One day in January of 1941, my sister Jean and I were walking along Main Street. We were returning to work after having lunch at home. She briefly stopped to talk with a friend who I found was very attractive. Having thought I already knew her, Jean didn't introduce me. I found myself gazing at her with the hope that one day we could get better acquainted. As we went on our way back to work at the bank I asked, "Who was *that*?" Jean seemed surprised that I didn't know her since they were both in the same small graduating class. She replied, "That was Geraldine Sutherland."

Well, from that time on I was determined to get a date with such a delightful young lady! This was the beginning of a lifetime relationship, for she eventually became my wife. When I first called her she was not very enthused, probably because she had heard of all the girlfriends I had had in high school. But with a lot of persistence, I finally got a date with her.

For our first date we went ice skating in a rink that used to be near the Kanawha City Bridge, across the river from Charleston. Neither of us could skate very well but that didn't discourage us. Maybe that's why I chose doing this activity since we had to hold on to each other in order to stay upright!

Dad was generous with letting me borrow his car. We began steady dating after this first date doing things like going on hayrides, hiking, swimming, and going to church and youth activities. Sometimes we even went with my family to Ritter Park or Camden Park in Huntington along with Hawks Nest, a gorgeous scenic area in the mountains east of Charleston. As we became better acquainted, my family nicknamed her "Gerry" but she was still known as Geraldine in her family.

An Extended Engagement

During the summer of 1941 we became engaged. I asked Dad to order the rings I had picked out from a jewelry catalog he had at the store. When the rings arrived I could hardly wait to put the engagement ring on her finger. I had Dad put the wedding ring in the safe until we needed it. This accomplished, we began to plan for a late fall wedding, maybe about Thanksgiving. How excited we were in those innocent days!

Well, things didn't go as planned. That fall I received my selective service draft notice informing me that I would have to spend a year in military service. Needless to say we both were very disappointed to have to postpone our wedding since we thought it best to wait until the year of service was completed.

The news during my high school days was of the war that was brewing in Europe. In my mind this seemed so far away and it just couldn't affect us. My Uncle Lewis Bird was a private in the Infantry in France during World War I, "The war that was to end all wars!" So this couldn't happen again, I thought.

The United States didn't want to be involved in war again but there were those who didn't want us to be caught without some defense against an invasion of our country. So, the Selective Training and Service Act was signed on September 16, 1940. This began the draft of men, between the ages of eighteen and thirty-seven, to be trained for the military service.

Our family store in St. Albans, WV

Top: Inside our family store; Dad is the fifth adult from
the right, wearing a light, three-piece suit with tie.
(Notice the inset charge slip on the lower right.)
Bottom: Dad's first car; I am the first one on the left.

CHAPTER 2

Entering the War

The deep recesses of my mind have been stimulated as I think back to my participation in World War II. Most of the major events of the war have not been forgotten; though I have tried to block out some of the unpleasant scenes. My involvement was not, I am sure, as intense as many in the infantry experienced. For instance my good friend from St. Albans West Virginia, Jim Stone, was in the marines and was severely injured while on one of the Islands in the Pacific war zone. For me it was just as much mental as it was traumatic.

Our country was just coming out of the Great Depression during the 1930s—1940s. Our President, Franklin Delano Roosevelt, had initiated some programs collectively known as the New Deal.

As for me, a young man of age twenty-one, I was dreaming of the day when life could really take on some significantly important things like getting married and having a family. During the 1930s, Adolph Hitler had been systematically invading all the countries in Europe. At the same time, he was executing those individuals he didn't think suitable for his own agenda. With all the atrocities of the holocaust and the suppression or slaughter of millions who opposed him, the question was, *who was going to stop him?*

As I frantically peered out the tiny window of the train, trying to get one last glimpse of my family, I could see Geraldine standing on her tiptoes and giving one final wave as we pulled out of the station. I was now leaving behind my somewhat sheltered life in this small, close-knit West Virginia town.

I arrived at Covington, Kentucky, Saturday night and was put on a truck, which shortly arrived at the Ft. Thomas military base.

First Taste of Army Life

My first taste of army life was at Fort Thomas, across the Ohio River from Cincinnati, Ohio, where I was given my uniform that was all wrinkled and reeked of moth balls. We also received lots of basic instructions and indoctrinations of army life. Fort Thomas was an induction center during WWI and WWII, where over eighty-thousand troops were signed up for military duty.

I remember my first time serving on KP (kitchen patrol) in the mess hall (officers' dining room). Everything, including floors, tables and chairs, had to be cleaned spick and span. Then there were the endless close-order drill practices, having to endure the not-so-kind drill sergeants, the large barracks, the crackling of the heating system, the cold showers and total lack of privacy.

On November 30, I was thrilled to see my parents who had driven all the way to see me. Along with them was my oldest sister Jean and Gerry, my Sweetheart. They, of course, couldn't stay long since Dad had to return to St. Albans to be at work the next morning.

Training for Extended Military Service

From Kentucky I was sent by train to Aberdeen Proving Grounds, Maryland, for basic training, arriving on December 6, 1941. It was such a cold winter that as I was standing on guard duty one night it seemed even colder than normal to me. Pulling KP and close-order drill or the endless training sessions were much preferred to this. I just never could seem to get warm enough. But whenever I was on guard duty the main task I had to do was to make sure the furnace for our building had enough coal.

I vividly remember the very next day Sunday, December 7. I was returning from the mess hall to the barracks when I heard from the loud speakers that 'The JAPANESE HAVE BOMBED PEARL HARBOR, HAWAII." I thought for a minute, *Pearl where?* I had never heard of the place. I suppose almost everyone knows now where Pearl Harbor is.

The next day, December 8, President Franklin Delano Roosevelt and the United States Congress declared war on Japan. This, of course, brought many changes for me. Now it meant that I would have to stay in the service until the war ended. Most of all, it changed our plans for marriage. We had no choice but to wait until the war ended, whenever that would be.

The following day President Franklin Roosevelt, addressing a joint session of Congress, called December 7 "a date which will live in infamy." Declaring war against Japan, Congress ushered the United States into World War II and forced a nation, already close to war, to abandon isolationism. Within days, Japan's allies, Germany and Italy, declared war on the United States, and the country began a rapid transition to a wartime economy in building up armaments in support of military campaigns in the Pacific, North Africa, and Europe.

Being from West Virginia, I read with keen interest an article in the *Charleston Daily Mail* about the Battleship West Virginia. It sadly described how the *USS West Virginia*, stationed in Pearl Harbor at the time of the attack, had been sunk by several bombs and torpedoes. Over a hundred lives on board the ship at the time were lost. (Interestingly, the *USS West Virginia* was resurfaced, repaired, and re-commissioned. It re-entered the war in 1944.)

It was Christmas, December 25, at Aberdeen and very quiet. Of course it was still very cold. I acquired a rare weekend pass to go to New York City and got to see the Empire State Building and General Grant's tomb among a few other sights.

Then for New Year's Day, I, along with a few other soldiers, was invited to a home for dinner. After the home-cooked meal they offered each of us a carton of cigarettes but I declined for I did not smoke.

I was on duty practicing drills one day when to my surprise the drill sergeant told me I had visitors. It was my uncle Walter Harper, my aunt Mary, my fiancée Geraldine, and Mom. They only stayed an hour or so and then had to head back home to St. Albans. Even though the visit was brief, I was so happy to see them again!

My Grandfather – Baxter Leland Bird

A few days later, January 11, 1942, I received a phone call from home telling of the death of my maternal grandpa, Baxter Bird. I was so saddened not only to lose him but also to hear the news being so far from home. Somehow I managed to be granted a three-day pass to go to his funeral.

Travel was slow in those days, and I knew I would have to hurry to make it home and back to Aberdeen in the allotted time. I hitchhiked to Baltimore and then to the airport. American Airlines had a flight to Charleston, West Virginia, by way of Washington, DC, and Philippi, West Virginia. The view from the plane was breathtaking as I looked down on the snowy mountain tops. My breath made the windows fog up but still I tried to get my first glimpse of the airport close to home. This was my first ride on a bigger plane. I had ridden on Geraldine's brother's plane before but that was much smaller.

The Charleston airport at that time was called Wertz Field, located near the town of Institute, across the Kanawha River from South Charleston. (Later a chemical plant built by Union Carbide was located on this property.) When I bought my ticket earlier that day, I lacked about ten cents having enough money but they let me have the ticket anyway since I was in my army uniform. Wertz Field was three miles from St. Albans, my destination. When my plane landed I didn't have any money left so started walking down the road where eventually someone stopped to pick me up. He dropped me off at the bridge in town, which was a toll bridge at the time. I needed to walk across but didn't have the five cents fare. The toll keeper knew me so let me pass by anyway. Another car picked me up and took me to my home on West Main Street. I was fortunate to arrive in good time, especially with all the help I received along the way.

It was so good to be home but sad to be parting with such a dear, loved one, my grandfather. Grandpa had gone to Miller's Meat Market on Second Avenue and while shopping died of a heart attack at the ripe old age of eighty-six. He was buried in Teays Hill Cemetery just a few yards above the entrance and just in sight of the Fairview Elementary School where I attended as a young boy. My grandmother continued to live with my uncle Lewis as she and my grandfather had done before his death.

After the funeral Dad drove me back to the airport and bought me a return ticket. Mom had also come along with Geraldine and her mother.

We said our sad goodbyes and somehow I arrived back at Aberdeen on time. Whew!

Upon returning to Aberdeen Proving Grounds I continued basic training. Tests were given for typing skills, mechanical aptitude and also an introduction to the many Articles of War. Finally, basic training was completed on January 29, 1942.

Several of us went by Pullman coach on the Pennsylvania Rail Road to my new assignment by way of St. Louis, Missouri, and then on to Camp Livingston, Louisiana, a camp that had been open since 1940. Travelling by truck we arrived at Pineville, twelve miles north of Alexandria, Louisiana. It was a treat to go from the cold winter in the north to a much sunnier warmer weather pattern in the south. My new assignment was to be a company clerk. I was now a private earning twenty-one dollars per month with room and board.

107th Maintenance Company

The 107th Ordnance Company from Pontiac, Michigan, was a Michigan National Guard Company that had been called up for active duty. An ordnance company usually had the job of supplying arms and ammunition to other groups. They also did the repair and upkeep of all the equipment, such as tanks, trucks, jeeps, and armament. We had several large machine shop trucks, instrument repair trucks, welding trucks, a kitchen truck, and twelve GM 6x6 trucks carrying duffle bags, extra clothing, office equipment and general supplies. Some of the trucks were for us to ride in while our company moved from place to place.

While at Camp Livingston, I had the opportunity to go to Alexandria, Louisiana, to attend a church service just one time. I went to the Baptist church and while there met the Miller family who took me home for Sunday dinner. The Millers were relatives of the Zerkles, some acquaintances from St. Albans, West Virginia, whom I knew before I was drafted.

I spent two months at Camp Livingston and during this time began learning the ropes, so to speak. Working in the office gave me experience along with one of the old hands before he was promoted to another task for the company. My job as company clerk was primarily to type the payrolls and keep the service records updated. Occasionally, I typed official correspondence for the company officers. Of course this was in addition to many other military duties. The camp was made up of tents that were about twelve-feet square. The bottom section was wood half way up with a screened section to the eaves and a canvas covering over that.

One day we were unexpectedly told we had to be trained to use a gas mask. We had to put on the mask, and then enter a building that had the gas turned on to make us aware of what the possibilities might be during our assignments in the war. I still remember how nasty the smell was and how it made you want to choke.

The 1941 Louisiana maneuvers were said to be the largest involving nineteen divisions and almost half a million men. They helped the military leadership try several kinds of strategies in battlefield conditions and create effective ways to handle the challenges they'd be experiencing in Europe while leading and providing for larger, combined combat units.

When I joined the company it was just completing maneuvers with the 32nd Infantry Division. Their whole division was in the process of leaving from various ports to the Pacific war zone. I found out some months later that just about all of them suffered injuries or death. We were much more fortunate.

Leaving Camp Livingston on April 1, 1942, we took three days for our motor convoy to make it along the gulf coast to Florida. We thought we were headed for Jacksonville, POE (Port of Embarkation) to the Pacific but that wasn't to be. The first night we camped at Gulf Port, Mississippi, the second night at Pensacola, Florida, and the third night at Tallahassee. But along the way our orders were changed, sending us to Camp Blanding, Florida, southwest of Jacksonville near Starke. For me it was such a relief not to be sent overseas so quickly.

Along the way I was one of several chosen to direct traffic one day. I was dropped off ahead of the convoy at an intersection and had to stand and point the direction to turn. I was sure glad they didn't forget to pick me up when my shift was over!

There was sandy soil at Camp Blanding and not as many trees like we had at Camp Livingston. The pine trees at Livingston were beautiful but Blanding had only a few scrubby pines. The tents were like those at

Livingston plus we had a nice lake in which to go swimming when we had time off.

The company cook did a great job of preparing our food while traveling. His truck was specially made with a way to prepare the food while moving. As meal time approached we pulled off the road at a convenient spot to eat.

Family Visit

April 26 to 28 I was excited that Gerry came with Mom and Dad and my sister Jean to visit. I was given a pass for those three days. We all visited the Oriental Gardens, Daytona Beach and stayed in a motel. It was so nice to go swimming in the Atlantic Ocean. I tried again to get her consent for marriage sooner but that was just wishful thinking, realizing we had to wait until after the war ended. As always, our precious time together passed quickly and the moment came much too soon to depart. On May 22, 1942, I was given two weeks of furlough and went home by train. I sure enjoyed seeing my family and friends.

Carolina Maneuvers July and August 1942

On July 4 we received orders to convoy to the Carolinas for maneuvers. We stopped on the way at Camp Stewart, Georgia, the first night; then at Ft. Jackson, South Carolina, the second night. On July 6 we arrived at Dilworth, North Carolina, and set up camp in the pines east of Wadesboro near route 74. While there the company was busy using the shop trucks as they made repairs on trucks or tanks and replaced damaged equipment.

It was here that I was promoted to (Corporal) Technician 5th Grade on July 11, 1942, but I didn't like being so close to West Virginia without being able to go home. Louise Pettus reported of the "Army War Games: The Carolina Maneuvers," (now available on Rootsweb). Pettus explains how nearly one-third of the entire US Army took part in these exercises, conducted in sixteen counties throughout the Carolinas from October 6 to November 30, 1941. She also said the Carolinas were chosen for these sites because they willingly welcomed the troops to their churches, homes, and civic organizations during their weekend breaks. We had to report for duty on Monday morning until Friday evening, when I went to a nearby town and stayed in a home, and on Sunday morning went to church with the host family. (Several years later my wife and I visited this family as we were on vacation on our way to Florida.)

Having finished our maneuvers, we headed back to Camp Blanding on August 16, spending one night at Camp Stewart, Georgia. Arriving at camp we were assigned to a new section that had larger wooden, more suitable barracks. During those warm evenings, I enjoyed a good swim, and then stopped at the PX (Post Exchange) to get some ice cream.

On September 23, I was given a ten-day pass to go home before going overseas, and traveled by Greyhound bus for twenty-four hours. This was the last time I would see my family until three long years later!

Enjoyed a family visit at Camp Blanding;
Top: With Mother and Dad; Bottom left: With Gerry;
Bottom right: With Mother and my sister Jean

Aberdeen Proving Grounds, Maryland;
Bottom left: Gas mask drill (Photos by FT)

Camp Livingston, Louisiana
Jan. 31, to April 1, 1942

Jan 31 1942 Assigned to 107th Ordnance Medium Maintenance Co., Camp Livingston, LA., by train to St. Louis, Mo. then to Alexandria, LA then to Camp Livingston. The 107th was on maneuvers with the 32nd Infantry Division which was training for action in the Pacific War Theater. Left Lousiana on April 1, 1942 for what we thought was to board a ship in Florida to Pacific

With the company flag at Camp Livingston, Louisiana

LOUISIANA TO FLORIDA - First Day April 2, 1942

REST STOP

Good view of SHOP TRUCKS

TIME TO EAT
Note: Officers eat at table. The rest eat on ground.

Notice the back view of the cook's truck on the lower left photo. Note also that the officers always had a table and chairs to sit on while the enlisted soldiers sat on the ground. (Photos by FT)

Time in Sunny Florida (Lighthouse and truck photo by FT);
Notice on the bottom right how the cook is standing
outside on the ledge while preparing food for the troops.

With Gerry at Camp Blanding

Rest Stop

Inside a Shop Truck

July 4 to Aug 16 -- CAROLINA MANEUVERS.

(Photos by FT)

My Tent

Supply tent

LOOK
AT MY
SLEEVE

BIVOUAC AREA
CAROLINA MANEUVERS
DILLWORTH, NORTH CAROLINA
JUL 6 TO AUG 15, 1942

Top: Visiting with family; Below: Training, training, training

The Queen Elizabeth, 11:00 a.m. on Nov. 30, 1942 in
Firth of Clyde, Glasgow, Scotland (Photo by FT)

CHAPTER 3

Crossing the Atlantic

After spending the rest of the summer in Florida, orders came for us to prepare for overseas duty. Military secrecy did not permit us to know where we were actually going until we boarded ship. Our entire company, with all of our equipment, went by train to Camp Kilmer New Jersey, arriving there on November 19, 1942.

Camp Kilmer

Camp Kilmer was the overseas staging area, thirty miles southwest of New York. The camp was named for the poet Joyce Kilmer, who enlisted as a private in World War I and rose to the rank of sergeant in the 165th Infantry. He was killed in action on July 30, 1918, in the Aisne-Marne offensive.

While there we were not permitted to call home or write anything of our movement. We spent a lot of time filling out forms and rechecking our equipment. Then we received passports, inoculations, and special training along with warnings about wartime in foreign countries. Being there only three days didn't allow us any spare time to look around the camp or even go to the PX to buy anything to take along with us. Soon we were put onboard a transfer ship that crossed over to New York harbor. It was now that the time had come to leave our homeland for an indefinite period of time.

New York Port of Embarkation

We boarded the troop ship *R.M.S. Queen Elizabeth* on November 22 at Pier 90 where I was assigned to sleep in a stateroom on "A" deck, room A-86. This room was normally for only two people but there were at least sixteen of us crammed in that tiny space! Overcrowding was an issue since there were eighteen thousand troops on board along with all of our equipment. The bathroom had only salt water for us to use and there were several other inconveniences that we had to get used to.

Two other large ships were in port at this time, the *Queen Mary* and the *Normandy*. It was quite a sight to sail by the Statue of Liberty on November 24 and be reminded of what we were fighting for. In the years to come I had to keep this image in my mind.

I slept very little over the next five days crossing the Atlantic. Besides, Captain Edward Bramston had volunteered our company for guard duty or watch, as it was called, when onboard a ship. I had to report for duty in the office that was set up in the upper forward deck with my job of maintaining communication and assigning troops for guard duty. This meant I didn't have any free time to explore the ship and even had to juggle sleeping and eating periods. I also had to stand in line to get any PX supplies I needed.

The *Queen* ships didn't travel in convoy with other ships having a fighter plane or gun boat escort because they were faster than any of the German U-Boats. That fact didn't stop us from being alarmed when suddenly one day a submarine alert was sounded while we were somewhere in the north Atlantic. Battle stations were manned and the adrenaline was flowing. Finally the all-clear sounded and we were told that we had evidently out run the submarine. Whew! I was reminded of Psalm 46:1, "God is our refuge and strength, an ever-present help in trouble" (NIV). And He did protect us all the way!

Also, somewhere near Iceland we went through a huge storm. The waves were so bad that the bow of the ship literally came up out of the water making the whole ship vibrate from the spinning propellers. Between the storm and the greasy mutton they fed us almost everyone was seasick. The ship was manned by the British crew so we had to eat British food. They served meals day and night. But there were so many of us on board that we only had two meals every twenty-four hours. Our journey across the ocean seemed both never-ending and all-too-quick at the same time. It seemed never-ending because of the discomforts we all felt that made us want to be on shore. However, being on shore meant we had to be ready for the unknown.

MESSING CARD

"A" MESS HALL

2 SECTION

FIRST MEAL 8-00 a.m.
SECOND MEAL 5-00 p.m.

Two meals of Mutton per day

KEEP THIS CARD
SLEEPING QUARTERS

ROOM **A** 86

ARRIVED 5 DAYS LATER AT 4:30
FIRTH OF CLYDE, SCOTLAND

(Photo by FT)

Top: Tower Bridge, London, and Barrage Balloons (Photo by FT)
Bottom: Exploring Stonehenge

CHAPTER 4

Stationed with the Brits

Jolly Old England and Meaningful New Friends

We arrived in the Firth of Clyde, Glasgow, Scotland on November 29, 1942. The *Queen* ship was so large that it couldn't dock in port, but at least it was safer out in the harbor. They off-loaded us onto a ferry, which took us to the docks.

As we left on this ferry to the shore I was curiously looking for any sight of land or anything of interest. Thankfully, the ferry turned sharply just enough for me to see several ships so I quickly took my camera from my pocket and was able to take a photo of the Queen ship. An officer and several men were to follow with all of our vehicles and duffle bags.

After disembarking we were put on a jam-packed train, which headed south. Overcrowding seemed to be the norm these days. We arrived at a British army camp at Tidworth, England, the next morning. Tidworth was just north of Salisbury and eighty miles west of London. We were put in the barracks named "Matthew" with army designation, Depot 0-640. We had the task of servicing and then shipping all of the equipment needed for the troops in North Africa. We had the use of the large shops that had equipment for handling our big tanks, trucks and jeeps that needed any repairs after inspections. Also many jeeps were assembled there and parked all over the hillside.

Hitler's air strikes were numerous during the year we were at Tidworth. Usually it would be in the middle of the night interrupting our sleep. Late one night when the air raid siren was blaring, we went up on the hillside behind our camp to practice using a fire pump. The hose was attached to the pump that was over a well but only five of us were able to successfully get the pump working. We sure didn't get much sleep during these strikes!

My task was to be ready to man the fire pumps in case we were bombed and some of the buildings were ablaze. This never happened, thankfully. While there, I was promoted to sergeant (Technician 4th grade) on July 5, 1943.

I visited Salisbury several times and went to a Baptist church on Sundays. Often I would be invited into homes of church members to visit and sometimes share a meal.

The first weekend after arrival I went with a truckload of soldiers to an USO show in Salisbury, featuring a movie star named Martha Rae. This was the only USO show I saw while overseas. We were ushered in and seated on the last seats available, on the front row. How nice to be able to see her up close! But before I sat down I heard my name being called from further back in the huge crowd. I immediately recognized Delmer Turley, my good friend from St. Albans! Neither of us knew the other was in England. He was stationed just west of Salisbury, so we were able to see each other occasionally. He was with the engineer branch of the army.

On my visits to the historic sites of England I witnessed the many barrage balloons ahead. For our protection from enemy air raids, these large blimps were used in many of the major cities. The blimps were tethered with metal cables. Low flying planes would fly into the cables and be disrupted. Some cables even had explosive devises attached, causing damage and often destroying enemy planes. Obviously, they didn't do much to deter higher flying aircraft.

During one of my many visits to Salisbury while in Tidworth, England, I was able to tour the beautiful Salisbury Cathedral, also called the Cathedral Church of the Blessed Virgin Mary. I found this Anglican church to be such an interesting place as I studied the tall spire, said to be the tallest in all of England, and became fascinated with the many gorgeous sculptures inside this enormous structure that was several stories tall. The many rooms inside were beyond description. I even saw tombs of the Crusaders, and ancient manuscripts, housed in the archives. I learned that the main structure was built between 1220 to 1258, but it was still in amazing shape.

V-Mail or Victory Mail

Many of us became discouraged with the mail system during early days of the war. It often took months for a letter to arrive from home, or for our loved ones to hear from us. We understood that necessary military supplies took precedence in limited shipping space, but the slow communication sure seemed unacceptable.

Much to our delight, the post office came up with a brilliant and workable solution. A limit of one eight-by-ten-inch sheet of paper was allotted to each soldier per day. The letter on this sheet was then microfilmed. Only the collected microfilms were shipped, and then reproduced in paper on the receiving end. This method was called V-Mail, for victory mail.

Happily, this shortened the time of delivery to an average of two weeks, and made a significant impact on the positive morale of all of us. How well I remember both sending and receiving the all-important V-Mail messages during the days of war.

A Visit to Stonehenge

Bicycles were available at the camp so, many times, I rode the fifteen miles to Salisbury instead of riding the bus.

I had heard about Stonehenge and read about it in military booklets. So one day while off duty, two or three of us decided to go by bicycle to see it. At that time all we had to do was open the gate and walk around and even climb on some of the giant stone slabs, although we didn't have any way to get on top of the tall, upright ones.

It was such an interesting site. Apparently, it is still a mystery how these huge stones were lifted or even exactly where they came from. Of course, today, it would be easy to lift them with cranes. (See photo at beginning of chapter.)

> Begun around 2800 BC, [Stonehenge] is one of the earliest sites in Great Britain. With the stones averaging in weight of some 40 tons each, it is difficult to imagine how they were brought to this site. More remarkable...is how they precisely align with the sky during the winter

and summer solstice, and each of the twelve months
(Hauck, p. 309, used with permission.)

Everything was so different in England. Driving on the left side of
the narrow roads was a challenge. Our large tanks and trucks (Lorries,
as they were called by the British) soon began to be made wider. We
had to repair many of the hedgerows and fences. The language seemed
strange to us and the currency took us some time to get familiar with.
For instance, when I boarded a bus, the conductor would say the fee was,
"Thrup'ence ap'ney" that is: three and one-half pence. The buses were
fueled by burning charcoal or peat in a burner on the outside beside
the motor. The gases were then fed into the motor. This didn't produce
very much horsepower and often we would have to get off a bus before
it reached the top of the hill. We walked up then waited for it to reach
the top before re-boarding. At least we didn't have to push the bus uphill.

A funny thing happened one evening at the barracks. There was a
man in the building who had a really bad case of foot odor. Several of
the men picked him up and carried him against his will to the shower
room, scrubbing his smelly feet with a brush while also using lye soap.
I didn't smell those bad feet ever again!

I went one time to visit the town of Bournemouth, on the English
Channel, which was a resort town in peacetime. At the Red Cross club
I met a man who invited me to go to church with him. There I met
and was befriended by the vicar, Reverend Rowdon and his wife. They
invited me to come and spend a night with them whenever I could. That
was such a delightful experience away from the army base life. They had
a large, beautiful home with a maid. The maid, without my knowing
it, took my boots during the night and by the next morning had them
outside my door all polished, better than what I could have done myself.

Weapon Inspections

Once in a while we would have weapons inspections. These were
usually just routine, but one time they had everyone in the 107th company
to lineup with our rifles. We had been instructed to always be sure to
have a very light coat of gun oil in the barrel in case we were in damp
places. So with a call for inspection on this occasion, as the officers

passed all around us, they were taking notes. When finished they called for several of us to step forward. We were pleased when they announced that we would be given a three-day pass to do anything we wanted to. I was able to choose to go visit the west coast of England to Wales.

I travelled to London on several occasions and usually stayed in a Red Cross hotel or the USO servicemen's center. It was interesting walking the streets of this large old city and seeing sites such as Buckingham Palace, Trafalgar Square, and Piccadilly Circus. But much of my memory of London recalls that it was always cold and dreary looking.

Sgt. Forrest Thornton

Top: Buckingham Palace; Bottom: Salisbury Cathedral
(Photos by FT)

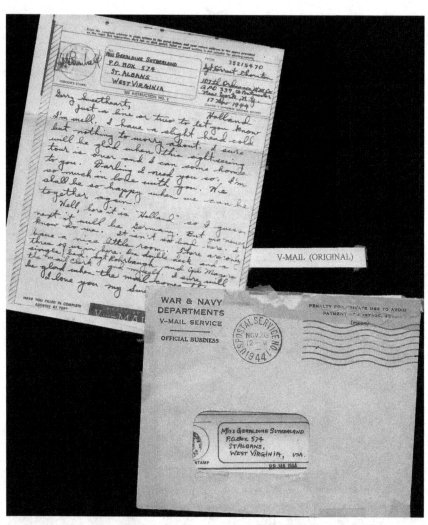

V Mail Letter to Gerry from FT (Photo by FT)

Edinburgh, Scotland (Photos by FT)

Sgt. Forrest Thornton in Great Britain

CHAPTER 5

Life in Great Britain

Devonshire and a Wedding

After almost a year at Tidworth we moved to the west coast town of Bideford, North Devon, on September 30, 1943. I became acquainted with several families when I visited the Baptist church in town, but the special one was the Langdon family. Later, I even attended the wedding of their daughter Evelyn who married Ronald Payne. (My wife, Gerry, and I made a trip to England and visited this couple forty-one years later in October of 1985; They were living in Leeds, Yorkshire, at the time.)

The Langdons treated me like I was one of their own. When I visited I could take canned food from the company mess hall to give to them, since I wouldn't be eating at camp. This meant a lot to them to supplement their meager supply of food. Their food as well as most necessities was rationed during the war. Their eyes would light up at the sight of canned or tins of vegetables and fruit. The children were also delighted with candy and gum I gave them. A common greeting from the children was, "Got any gum, Chum?"

I remember one time requesting some popcorn to be sent from my parents. After it came I took it with me for them to pop. Believe it or not they had never heard of popcorn! I showed them how to do it but when the grains started to pop they didn't know what to think. After the butter and salt was applied I took a bite then gave them some. At first they didn't like it, but later, after a few more bites, smiles broke out and they decided they did.

Shortly after our arrival at Bideford, an officer from our company and I drove back to Salisbury to pick up the payroll that had been processed for us. We were in the company staff car, a 1943 Ford four-door sedan. As we were nearing the city limits I had slowed up for traffic and noticed a man riding on a horse, fairly close to the road. As traffic was again moving I proceeded also. Just then the horse reared as he had been frightened at something and he ended up backing into our car. After several minutes passed we realized they seemed okay and the rider motioned for us go on our way. The next month's payroll was available closer to our camp so we didn't encounter any more excitement that time.

While at Bideford I established a friendship with US Army Sergeant Earl Daniel. He was with an ordnance heavy maintenance company. We got together at the Baptist church and at some of the church outings. We became good friends but soon had to part as we were headed into France. I didn't see him again until we met in Paris near the end of the war in Europe.

After my return home and subsequent marriage, Gerry and I went on our honeymoon in the Blue Ridge Mountains of Virginia. We decided to try to find Earl's parents' home. They lived on a farm outside of a small town called Gladys, Virginia. We found them and they expressed their delight in seeing us. They even insisted we take the main bedroom upstairs. Earl had not been discharged at this time and was still in Paris but he finally was discharged and eventually got married. We visited Earl and his wife, Pauline several times since then.

On the back of all my photos was a censorship stamp. I somehow found that the navy could get my photo film developed and printed with stamped verification along with a new roll of film, all for free. (See end of chapter for photo.)

Preparing for D-Day

The invasion of France, D-Day, would come on June 6, 1944. All combat units were poised and ready for action. Because there were so many US, Canadian, and British combat troop ships lined up for miles from the port of embarkation our company had to wait our turn. Besides our company was still busy equipping all the invasion units for the crossing of the channel. All the men in my company, the 107th Ordnance Company (a hundred and fifty troops in all), were ready to get on with the job we had been training to do during the past three years.

Waterproofing Tanks for Invasion

Finally the day came when we knew the equipment we were taking ashore was ready for the landing. For most of the year before this, our company, along with a few others, had been experimenting with water-proofing materials and sealants on all the equipment for the invasion. This took many hours of testing materials and methods to enclose the motors to prevent them from drowning out in deep water. The landing craft used for transporting tanks would not guarantee an easy or safe landing. A metallic material was used to cover the air intake and exhaust.

A near tragedy occurred with one such testing of a tank in the bay at Pebble Ridge near Bideford, North Devon. As the tide began to ebb, the sounding indicated a safe depth for the tank to be let off the end of the landing craft. When it did leave, it stood on end for what seemed an eternity. The sergeant on the tank later told me that there was an apparent dip or soft area in the sand where the tank debarked. After a few seconds of teetering back and forth with the waves it finally dropped with the topside up and went on shore safely.

During the months before D-Day, every unit going across the channel had to be instructed on how to waterproof its own equipment. We knew invasion was imminent because one day as I was driving my jeep along the west coast of England I saw a magnificent sight. Everywhere as far as the eye could see were ships and landing craft of all description. What a sight that was! This was one of the many staging areas for the impending invasion. I had been overseas two years already so it could not come too soon for me!

We finally left Bideford on July 31 and headed south by Burns Hill Camp, later ending up at Hatch Beauchamp Camp. It was there that our company joined with Lieutenant General William Hood Simpson, Commander of the US 9th Army Group August 24, 1944, and we soon boarded the ship, James Caldwell, August 31, heading for France. All were under the supreme command of General Dwight David Eisenhower. I greatly admired Eisenhower, who would become a 5-star general, and later our thirty-fourth president of the United States.

Eisenhower (born October 14, 1890) was a graduate of the West Point Military Academy and served as a major in Panama and the Philippines. Early in 1942, General George Marshall, then Army Chief of Staff, appointed him chief of the operations division of the General Staff. In June of 1942, he was made commander of the American forces in Europe. In July, he was promoted to lieutenant general. His leadership in the successful invasions of Sicily, Italy, and finally in the dramatic D-day invasion of Normandy made him the symbol of freedom to all our allies. I received a copy of the following letter, written by General Dwight David. Eisenhower just as D-Day was beginning:

> You are about to embark upon the Great Crusade, toward which we have striven these many months. The eyes of the world are upon you. The hopes and prayers of liberty-loving people everywhere march with you. In company with our brave Allies and brothers-in-arms on other Fronts, you will bring about the destruction of the German war machine, the elimination of Nazi tyranny over the oppressed peoples of Europe, and security for ourselves in a free world. Your task will not be an easy one. Your enemy is well trained, well equipped and battle hardened. He will fight savagely. But this is the year 1944! Much has happened since the Nazi triumphs of 1940-41. The United Nations have inflicted upon the Germans great defeats, in open battle, man-to-man.
>
> Our air offensive has seriously reduced their strength in the air and their capacity to wage war on the ground. Our Home Fronts have given us an overwhelming superiority in weapons and munitions of war, and placed at our disposal great reserves of trained fighting men. The tide has turned! The freemen of the world are marching together to Victory! I have full confidence in your courage and devotion to duty and skill in battle. We will accept nothing less than full Victory! Good luck!

And let us beseech the blessing of Almighty God upon this great and noble undertaking.

Signed, D.D.E.

When Eisenhower penned this letter, he wasn't fully convinced he was making the right decision to invade Normandy.

HANDY CROSS CAMP BIDEFORD, N. DEVON, ENGLAND

MY OFFICE

ENTRANCE TO
←OUR CAMP
↓

JUNE 1944

RIFLE RANGE PRACTICE, WEST COAST FROM BIDEFORD, ENGLAND JULY, 1944

(Photos by FT)

My office and duty station at Pebble
Ridge, Bideford, England, 1943

Top: Ordnance Company on parade;
Bottom left: Water-proofed tanks (Photos by FT)

At my pup tent ("French Villa") in 1944

CHAPTER 6

D-Day, France

Normandy Landings and Utah Beach

Carrying full equipment, American assault troops moved onto Utah Beach as early as September 4, 1943, nine months before the invasion of Normandy. Utah Beach was in the area defended by two battalions of the 919th Grenadier Regiment. Members of the 8th Infantry Regiment of the 4th Infantry Division were the first to land, arriving at 06:30. Their landing craft were pushed to the south by strong currents, and they found themselves about two-thousand yards from their intended landing zone. This site turned out to be better, as there was only one strongpoint nearby rather than two, and bombers of the 9th Bomber Command had bombed the defenses from lower than their prescribed altitude, inflicting considerable damage. In addition, the strong currents had washed ashore many of the underwater obstacles. The assistant commander of the 4th Infantry Division, Brigadier General Theodore Roosevelt, Jr., the first senior officer ashore, made the decision to "start the war from right here," and ordered further landings to be re-routed.

It is impossible to describe my inner feelings as I anticipated our destination of landing on Utah Beach. The report of thousands who had died trying to establish a beachhead was on my mind. The storm that had been raging on and off for some days had begun to lighten up.

We disembarked from the *Liberty* ship onto an LCT at 9:00 am. Our landing craft bobbed up and down on the waves as we approached the coast of Normandy and I was filled with anxiety. Our landing on Utah Beach on September 4 was rather quiet since the allied troops had established control for several miles inland. We passed through several towns then stopped at 3:30 pm at Periers. I slept uneasily most of the night under a heavy downpour of rain. The next day we went on to our destination of MiForet', ten miles north of Rennes, France.

Field Marshal Montgomery was head of ground forces and (as mentioned before) General Eisenhower was Supreme Commander of the Allied Expeditionary Forces. The plan called for an amphibious invasion of the French coast and an advance into Germany. The Allies made a paratroop and amphibious assault on the Normandy peninsula between LeHavre and Cherbourg at dawn on June 6, 1944 as more than a hundred-and-sixty-thousand troops landed along a fifty-mile stretch. Despite heavy losses, the allies were able to hold and expand their beachhead. At the same time, allied air power played a vital part by breaking German communications and giving support to ground troops with the myriad of ships engaging in this same mission.

Allied bombers made more than eleven-thousand attacks, and approximately five-thousand ships joined the operation (The Houston Chronicle, Sunday, April 3, 1994). Sadly, the human cost was high. Over nine-thousand allied troops were wounded or killed, but because of their sacrifices over a hundred-thousand others were able to begin the march across Europe, to defeat Hitler's war machine (http://www.army.mil/d-day/index.html).

Our Company finally left Bideford on July 31, and went to Burns Hill Camp just three miles from Taunton. August 5 we arrived at Hatch Beauchamp just six miles southeast of Taunton. I visited with my friend Delmer Turley for a brief time on August 14 and 15 at Winchester and we enjoyed comparing war stories.

We left August 29 for Southampton and boarded the SS James Caldwell on August 31. Crossing the channel was rough with bad weather. This made us thankful to finally be boarding a landing craft which we anchored over night near the White Cliffs of Dover. Next morning we headed toward France. Still the weather was very stormy as we neared our destination so we anchored for two more nights.

France's Towns and Cities Along the Way

Along the way, I experienced many towns and cities throughout the country of France. On our first night there, the rains were so heavy our pup tents got drenched. Some spent the night in shop trucks but I slept underneath one myself.

Many of the places we went to after that included: Utah Beach, Sainte-Mère-Église, LaHavre DuPuits, Lassay, Periers, St. Sauveur, Gavray, LaHavePesnel, Avranches, LaCroix, Ramazy, StAubin, Chevaigne, and MiForet. Later, we also traveled through Rennes, Paris, Longiuneau, Longuyon, and Maastricht.

I called my pup tent in France, My French Villa. While there I remember voting for my first time in the presidential election. This was won by President Franklyn D. Roosevelt for his third term.

My office was in a building behind my tent (see picture at the beginning of this chapter). Again we were faced with learning a new kind of money for our pay, called Franks. Just in back of this camp location there was a large ammunition dump beside the railroad.

The Infantry began to push the Germans out of France and back toward Germany, making it safer for us to move our big trucks on across France to the Belgian-Dutch border.

We circled to the south of Paris and then on to a place near Maastrict, Holland. Before we arrived to the city we were told to disburse in a large apple orchard which became our home for three long rainy days. Every day it was the same; each morning pack up our pup tent and be ready, then each evening unpack for another night. During those few days everything we owned was saturated from the rain and mud.

So all we did was sit and wait. To break the monotony I had even thought about climbing some of the trees to get an apple to eat but on second thought climbing up a wet tree with water running down the back of my neck was not very appealing. Besides, the apples were so sour and bitter that even the worms and the birds couldn't eat them. During these long wearisome days all I could do was think of the warm, dry comforts of home sweet home.

One day when the weather had cleared enough I took the following photo. It was such an amazing sight to see all the vapor trails from the allied bomber raids over us as they headed toward Germany.

Top: The Siegfried Line on the Belgian border as
we entered Germany - built during WWI;
Bottom: Dec. 25th Theater for the night (Photos by FT)

CHAPTER 7

Belgium, Holland, and the West European Campaign

Now, it was time to experience Belgium and Holland. In Belgium, we passed through the towns of Hasselt, Rijkel, Vielsalm, Verviers, Liege, Lamur, Grmonster, Brussels, and Antwerp. While in Holland, we went through Maastricht and Heerlen.

The infantry began to push the Germans out of France and back toward Germany, making it safer for us to move our big trucks across France to the Belgian-Dutch border. All along the way there was evidence of the fierce fighting that had paid its toll. Many cities were completely leveled to the ground and dead animals and people were all around. Even in some places the trees on sides of the hills were barren of leaves from the artillery fire. It looked as if a forest fire had cleaned it out.

On November 16, 1944, we went to Heerlen, Holland for a month. We occupied the buildings of a school and scout camp. While there I befriended the Daemens, a Dutch family who lived across the street. On my visits neither of us could understand each other's language, so we used hand signals and gestures. We seemed to be able to communicate okay.

Here again we regularly heard the many air raids and bombs flying by over our heads. I vividly remember how a German plane was shot down by our air force. It passed right over our building and crashed and burned just several yards from us. All of us looked out of the office window as the pilot parachuted to the ground and then was apprehended. Many of the buildings across the street from our barracks had pock marks on the brick or stone walls made by our planes and enemy fire.

After having our evening meal our cook would bang two pans together to make a loud noise. Upon hearing this, the children in the area caught on so it became a signal that there was some leftover food. They came running with their little pots or pans and the cook dished out portions of food to each one who came. The food was all mixed together in their containers yet they returned to their homes delighted with another meal.

West European Campaign (1944-1945)

The allies tried unsuccessfully to take the Siegfried Line (a German defensive line also called by Germans the West Wall) from the rear by a combined air-borne and ground force strike across the Meuse, Waal, and lower Rhine rivers in Holland. A general offensive all along the line from Holland to Switzerland began in mid-November. The key points of Metz, Belfort, and Strasbourg were taken, local penetrations were made in the Aachen and Saar regions, and the Rur River was reached.

We shuffled back and forth between towns such as Masseik and Hasselt, Belgium, and Heerlen and Maastricht, Holland. It was here that we were on the front lines, constantly enduring many air raids, artillery shells and buzz bombs day and night. Liege, Belgium was the main target, being the direct supply point for all the American front lines. While here I also had my first taste of ice cream in over two years!

World War II: V-1 Flying Bomb (Military History)

Of interest to me was the forerunner of today's drone, the flying bomb. Germans first had the idea as early as 1939. After heavy losses in 1942, the German air force decided to do their best to turn this idea into a reality. They later created a successful weapon with a hundred-fifty-mile range. The V-1 flying bomb was a simple explosive rocket, propelled by a small jet engine and directed by an automatic pilot to a predetermined target (militaryhistory.about.com; http://www.army. mil/d-day/index.html).

One of the most frightening encounters was hearing and then seeing the first of many German buzz bombs. These pilotless, jet-propelled planes were flying bombs and were highly unpredictable. They would sometimes suddenly drop straight down and explode. Others would glide for miles after the motor quit before hitting a target. The psychological impact was as real as the destructive force. One such buzz bomb was so low as it passed overhead the leaves were rustling in the trees. It went on several miles before exploding.

These sightings became more regular as we neared the Rhine River. We could count off every quarter hour by their appearance day and night for several weeks. This was not a good morale builder. Again, I said to myself, *Will the war never end?* I suppose these were the darkest days of the war for me.

One day as I was in the office working on the company records while the rest of the men were in some nearby buildings repairing damages to equipment, I heard someone enter. Thinking it was one of ours I didn't look up. Then a voice commanded, "Soldier, stand up!" I couldn't believe it when I saw that an officer, a major, was facing me. Stunned, I jumped to my feet and saluted him. He asked where the captain was. Of course, he was busy somewhere there on the compound. I nervously accompanied the major and found our captain with the men. What the major did next seemed preposterous. He had all of us stand in line then told us to clean up some of the mess that the Germans had left. Such a big deal about nothing!

We were only there for two days then received orders to retreat, for the Germans were making a push back into the area. We quickly packed everything and left as it was getting dark. Along the way there was still some danger of German planes flying low, ground attacks using their guns and then flying back upward. This was called strafing. Thus, all lights had to be turned off except the small blackout lights, which had to be used on all vehicles traveling at night. Driving through towns was not only dangerous but scary. Finally, we found a safe place to hide for the night.

These blackout lights were both head and tail lights with unique lenses throwing only a thin, horizontal light to oncoming or approaching vehicles. They were used for night-time convoys in enemy territory.

This was during the Battle of the Bulge when we were being pushed back and forth several times, wondering would we ever break on through to the Rhine River.

We realized we were dead-center of the German offensive called the Bulge. Because the Nazis were trying to take Liege, Belgium, which was one of the main supply points for our front lines, we had to retreat for some miles back into Belgium.

On guard duty

ALLIED BOMBERS HEADED FOR GERMANY

ALUMINUM FOIL DROPPED BY OUR
BOMBERS TO DEFLECT GERMAN RADAR

Notice the sliver of aluminum foil on the lower
right of the picture. (Photo by FT)

Top: Sporting my new field jacket;
Bottom: Sgt. Forrest Thornton beside a German
plane that had just crash landed

CHAPTER 8

Battle of the Bulge, Germany

Up until now I had thought we had exhausted all of the unusual sleeping quarters but I was wrong. By December 20, we were in Palenburg, Germany, where we spent three days and nights. Our housing was unusual as we stayed in the coke ovens where they had heat and electric lighting. The 'coke' made in these ovens was a solid fuel made by heating coal in the absence of air so that the volatile components could be driven off. This one was not being used at the time we were there.

Outside it was freezing cold of course and snow was everywhere. Years afterward I could feel any cold weather in my ears from the frostbite I received while there since I had to spend much of my time outdoors.

A Dangerous Spot for Guard Duty

I'll never forget one night being so dark I couldn't see the hand in front of my face as I was doing guard duty. When the sergeant of the guard placed me he ordered, "Don't move from this spot!" I really didn't understand or appreciate why he had said this until the next morning on the next tour of duty. I saw that immediately in front of where I stood the night before was a huge crater full of water that had been created by a bomb. "The Lord is my shepherd, I lack nothing. He makes me lie down in green pastures, he leads me beside quiet waters" (Psalm 23:1-2, NIV).

During this time, German soldiers dressed in US uniforms began parachuting behind our lines. They could speak English fairly well and this was confusing at best. But with a special password issued each day for identification we could soon detect if they were one of us or not--that is if they hadn't already shot us in the meantime. We were now dead-center of the German offensive called the Battle of the Bulge.

It was now December 25, my fourth Christmas away from home and the third one overseas. I was very homesick and discouraged thinking I would never make it back home. We spent the night in an abandoned theater building where the seats had been taken out to allow us floor space to sleep. At least we were inside, out of the miserably cold weather. It was then that I wrote the following letter to my fiancé, Gerry.

My Christmas Letter from Belgium, December 25, 1944

Dear Darling Gerry,

As I write this letter I realize that you will not get it for about a month or so. But I want to let you know I am okay and how it is here in Belgium on this cold winter day. And to let you know am safe and that "I love you."

I must say that I miss you terribly and long for the day when this war will be over. This being the third Christmas overseas makes me think that the war will never end. I find myself dreaming of the time when, if ever I get home, we can get married and have Christmas in our own home.

Since you know I cannot write much about what is going on at this time here or particularly where I am, I will have to use generalities. We were fortunate to find a safe and dry place for this Christmas Eve. We are in an old abandoned Theater that has all the seats removed. I have my bedroll in a nice spot so hope to get a good night's rest.

We have been on the road for two days now. We received orders that we would no longer be with the Ninth US Army but now being assigned to General Omar Bradley's First US Army. I have heard by the grape vine that some of the first armored units with tanks are poised to make it across the Rhine River and into Germany.

My captain was at a place called Remagen and said there were rumors that they were ready to take the bridge.

There were a lot of anxious moments a few weeks ago as we were in the thick of it in the Ardennes Forest area of Belgium. We had to retreat several miles for the Bulge was moving in on us. We can't afford to be too close to the front lines because of the valuable repair trucks with all the equipment to fix broken vehicles and armory. Our welders have had a hay day in that they found a factory with stacks of armor plate. They made some tank crews happy when they welded an extra thickness of steel to the front of their tanks.

Getting back to this evening; one of the fellows in our company has a guitar so we often gather around and sing favorite songs. In fact we are singing Christmas carols right now. Oh, the memories it brings back to the times in the good old USA when Mom and Dad would do their best to make Christmas a happy time for us six children.

Last Christmas, 1943 I was in Bideford, England and was on guard duty in charge of quarters. So didn't get to visit my friends, the Langdons, but did so that weekend. It was nice to get out of base camp but it still was a very lonely time away from home and family.

Someone just found out that one of the curtains this old theater has for the stage could be let down and it is so colorful. We don't have a tree but with the music and lights and warmth of the building it helps to pass the time.

This night should be safer than a few days ago. We had moved into a captured town about midnight and each of us scattered to find a place to sleep for the night in Vielsalm, Belgium. I climbed up some stairs in the dark, and found inside what looked like an apartment above some abandoned shops. I spread my bed roll and spent the night but was awakened in the morning with snow falling on my head. The roof had been previously destroyed by bombs.

Enough of my ramblings, I do hope you don't have to work the switchboard this evening. Does the Phone Company make you work nights any longer? I would love to be able to meet you after work and take you home. Are your mother and dad taking it well with your brother deciding to go into the Navy? How is Woodford? Is he still flying bombers in the Pacific?

How are you getting along with the piano and voice lessons? I would love to hear you.

Sorry this letter is so long but with each passing day hopefully the day will come when I can come home. I'm glad to be able to serve my country, though it is tough to be gone so long without seeing you or being able to talk with you.

Your last letter was so good telling of the good time with family at Thanksgiving at your grandmother's, I would love to have been there with you.

Remember, I love you and will be home before too long, hopefully.

All my love and kisses. . . Your- loving Sweetheart, Forrest

PS: Thanks for the scripture verses on your letters, they are so meaningful. It is hard to find time to even open my Gideon New Testament and concentrate on what I read. And thanks for your prayers.

We haven't had church services very often with our moving about so much. A Chaplain will once in a while come along and hold service for us.

Now I need to join the others with the singing.

With all my love, Forrest
(Props as I write: – a chair, small table, a sleeping bag, and my army shoulder bag and my Carbine)

==

[Envelope] From: Sgt. Forrest Thornton
107th Ordnance MM Company
APO 505 c/o postmaster New York, NY
To: Miss Geraldine Sutherland
P.O. Box 574
St. Albans, WV

New Assignment – the First U.S. Army

We had just been re-assigned to the First US Army under General Omar Nelson Bradley of the Twelfth Army Group. This was the beginning of the Battle of the Bulge. News soon came that the Ludendorff Bridge at Remagen across the Rhine River had been crossed by some of our armored units, giving us renewed hope that we were winning.

The sudden capture of a bridge across the Rhine was front-page news in American newspapers and our military news. This allowed Commander Dwight David Eisenhower to change his plans to end the war. The bridge made way for us to be able to quickly move five divisions across the Rhine into the Ruhr, Germany's industrial area. The Ludendorff Bridge had endured months of aircraft bombing, direct artillery hits, and the deliberate demolition attempts to destroy it. The bridge finally collapsed on March 17th. Also by this time, twenty-eight US Army Engineers were killed and sixty-three were wounded. Eventually the army engineers succeeded in building several heavy duty bridges that made it possible to cross the Rhine.

Over twenty-five-thousand troops crossed into Germany before the Americans broke out of the bridgehead on March 25. This was eighteen days after the bridge had been captured. Captain Francis Gallagher made a scouting trip there but our company did not go then. A little later we crossed over the Rhine on one of the pontoon bridges the engineers had built.

The sounds of war continued. One of the sounds I suppose I will never forget was the ear shattering noises of our heavy artillery shells as they whined over our heads heading into Germany.

At a place called Fraiture Chateau, a chilling incident happened I have wondered about many times. I was stationed at the main gate entrance to our compound for guard duty. There was heavy snow on the ground with a bright moonlight. I could see several miles away and everything was quiet. All of a sudden I realized that an airplane coming from the German border was approaching on my left! The plane passed so close I could have hit it with a rock. My heart was beating so fast and the adrenalin was rushing! It definitely was a German plane in which I could clearly see the pilot and the swastika emblem on the tail of the plane!

After the plane passed on over beyond my view I heard some bombs exploding. I contemplated should I yell for the sergeant of the guard or just remain quiet! Then I remembered our orders were to not fire our rifle in a situation as this for fear of being killed. Sure enough I could hear the plane return over the same route but no bombs were dropped where we were stationed. I never made any remarks to anyone about what had happened. This was another example of how God protected me during this dangerous situation.

I remember looking out the window of my office and onto the street below. The buildings I saw had a lot of damage from bombings before we arrived at this small village. We arrived around midnight with each of us scattering with our bed-roll to possibly get some sleep. The next morning I was wakened by snow coming down from a bombed out roof above me. I certainly made sure I moved my bed-roll and slept in a better spot the next night.

Soon several tanks came by and stopped for repairs. We were fortunate that the men of our company had excellent abilities to do repair work on the weapons of war.

Battle of the Bulge

On December 16, 1944, the Germans started their Ardennes Offensive. After punching through the thin allied line in the Ardennes sector, they moved in a swift counteroffensive into Belgium, followed later by a thrust into Alsace.

Forces under Montgomery and Patton beat back the Germans in the Ardennes while the allied forces in Alsace held firm. The allies lost more men in the Battle of the Ardennes than in any other battle in the invasion of France and Germany. The battle was also tremendously costly for the Germans.

In terms of losses, the Battle of the Bulge, was certainly one of the worst. To begin with, record low temperatures struck the Ardennes Forest on the German-Belgium border. General George Patton even prayed on the Armed Forces radio network, asking God to give better weather for the oncoming combat. Interestingly, God seemed to honor that prayer (http://www.indianamilitary.org/).

The allies resumed their delayed offensive with a drive to the Rhine. Vigorous and rapids operations wiped out German resistance west of the Rhine and made bridgeheads on the east bank. A surprise offensive in the Saar crumbled the Siegfried Line defenses.

A Narrow Escape

This Bible verse applies to how the Lord was protecting me: "Even though I walk through the darkest valley, I will fear no evil, for you are with me; your rod and your staff, they comfort me" (Psalm 23:4, NIV). This is God's holy word.

There was another frightening experience while we were stationed just south of Bonn, Germany. I had previously left the company payroll there to be processed. We left early on a beautiful, sunny day, the temperature about freezing with deep snow on the ground. I was in a jeep with Lieutenant Jo Pinhero and our driver, Private Clarence Magers, going back to pick up the payroll.

We knew that the Germans had great freeways called the Autobahn. We decided to try to get on one for it would save us some time. So we spotted one to the right, which was on a rise high above us. Thinking this would be the quickest way we turned onto the road across a field in order to get up on it. Just about 1000 yards from the approach to the Autobahn an outpost guard stopped us. He asked for the password of the day and asked for our purpose in being there.

After we told the guard our intentions he informed us that just over the rise of the Autobahn his US Armored Division was preparing to challenge the Germans and was ready to cross over for a battle. Looking up at the top of the ridge we could see a truck that was burning. Shockingly he told us that the last ones that went up there had gotten shot. We quickly retraced our steps back to a safer road called the Red Ball Route. The Red Ball route enabled supplies to be quickly expressed to troops on the front (/ranschool.lee.army.mil.museum/transportation%20museum/redballintro.htm).

After receiving the payroll we returned to our base without getting injured. We had many close calls with the Germans but I thank the Lord that I never faced them directly.

Then Christmas came and we were reassigned to the headquarters forward unit of the First Army. This put us directly in front of the German drive during the Bulge. This also made it convenient for the repair work needed on the tanks and other equipment. Some of our trucks had run over land mines but thankfully none of the men of our company had any injuries except minor ones.

During these cold days we spent about a month at a place called Germonster Chateau. My office was set up in a room that was not, in my opinion, a good place for me to be. But somehow I got the charcoal burner going to make it comfortable enough to do some typing. After a little time I started smelling a very peculiar odor. I knew it wasn't me and I was not keen about looking under the floorboards for a dead body or animal! Several times I went outside to get a breath of fresh air then returned, almost wanting to hold my breath, to start over where I had left off. One day, out of curiosity and wondering where that horrible smell was coming from, someone came in and lifted some of the boards on the floor only to find a decaying animal of some sort that no one had ever seen before. The problem was solved but I guess it didn't matter since we left and moved to a different place several days later.

On February 20, 1945, we moved into a captured factory in Stolberg, Germany. It had tons of steel plates that had been used to make armor piercing bullets. If they could make it, our tanks, the US Sherman, would come back from battle with much needed repair. Some had to be carried back on a large flatbed truck called a tank retriever. The German Panzer tank had more fire power than ours with an 88mm cannon. Ours had a 90mm cannon.

One day a call came into my office for us to pick up a disabled US tank not too far from us. So, three of our men set out with their huge tank retriever. On a bleak back road they suddenly came face-to-face with a German tank! The adrenaline was rushing as our quick-thinking crew left their vehicle and hit the ditch. Fortunately one grabbed a bazooka before leaving the truck. These brave men managed to crawl close enough to fire the bazooka into the German tank, killing all on board. Thankfully our guys came back safely without a scratch!

I can't remember where this next strange event took place because we often were on the move to another location. As three of our men in a jeep were entering a small village they saw white sheets or pillow cases dangling out the windows. These of course were indication of surrender. But as the men moved a few yards along the road, the sheets suddenly disappeared. When they heard some shots being fired they quickly turned their jeep around and scooted back to camp. It must have been a setup but thankfully their quick thinking and the help from above aided them to escape unharmed.

A very unusual occurrence happened one day when a young man, who had escaped the Germans after his capture, entered our company area. Lo and behold, he turned out to be the young brother of Sergeant Ken Miles of our company! He was warmly greeted by all of us as we slapped him on the back, plaguing him with questions about his escape. Our sergeant didn't even know his brother was in the service! You can imagine the surprise of everyone at this coincidence!

As the snows began to melt there was an awful smell in the air. Many dead animals and men, who had been killed during the fierce battles were everywhere. The animals were beginning to swell up and burst. The retreating Germans had stripped those who had fallen of anything valuable, particularly their boots. I saw many of those bare feet sticking upward.

It wasn't at all unusual to see refugees trying to return to their homes or homeland. Either they would be walking or riding on an old wagon being pulled by horses or by hand.

K-Rations and Swine Flesh

A K-ration was the World War II version of a soldier's ready-to-eat meal on the field. It came in individually-wrapped packages for breakfast, lunch, or supper.

Our company cooks were very talented and could quickly stir up delicious meals, but this depended on available food supplies. Several very cold days left us without any way to get good meals. But somehow we found out that prepared food cartons were being air dropped. The

K-rations were what saved the day, and even came with a small Bunsen burner to heat the meals. I recall sitting on a snowy hillside trying out my K ration. This made a satisfying meal with pretty good food at this time for me.

One day while still in Germany it was discovered that a large supply of food became available. It was called swine flesh, which was some kind of well-prepared pork for a good meal. I'm sure I wouldn't care for it now, but at the time it was a nice alternative.

Death of President Roosevelt

On April 12, 1945, President Franklin Delano Roosevelt passed away at Warm Springs Georgia. His funeral procession was on April 14 in Washington DC, and he was buried at his Springwood estate in Hyde Park, New York. Harry Truman, being the vice president at this time, stepped into his shoes, finding that he had suddenly inherited all of the wartime problems.

Hitler's Death

Towards the end of the war the Russians, nearing the underground bunker under the Chancellery building in Berlin, Germany, discovered that Nazi leader Adolf Hitler had shot himself in the head with his pistol, likely after swallowing cyanide, ending his own life on April 30, 1945. In the same room with Hitler was his new wife, Eva Braun, who ended her life by also swallowing a cyanide capsule. After their deaths, SS men carried their bodies up to the Chancellery's courtyard, covered them with gasoline, and lit them on fire. Millions of people from around the world rejoiced that this evil man no longer lived!

Chaplain's Assistant, 83rd Ordnance Battalion

Proverbs 3:5-6 declare, "Trust in the Lord with all your heart and lean not on your own understanding; in all your ways submit to him, and he will make your paths straight" (NIV). And Proverbs 29:27a states, "The righteous detest the dishonest" (NIV).

These verses from the Holy Bible gave me confidence as the following happened in the Lord's wisdom for me to have made the right choice.

As it became evident that the war was about over, I chose to take a job as a chaplain's assistant for two months. This meant voluntarily giving up my sergeant rank for corporal, and of course, a pay cut. I had felt rather cooped up in my office and longed to be outdoors looking at the countryside. I deliberately have omitted giving the chaplains name to give him some respect.

I'm sure that Captain Gallagher looked at me solemnly before he granted the request to be reduced from sergeant to corporal. This turned out to be an interesting experience, though not very spiritual. My job was to play the little field pump organ for church services. I cannot remember any of the chaplain's sermons but it seems like most of them were repeated several times with different audiences.

We drove to an area where it would be suitable to have a service for any soldiers who came. It was usually out in a wooded area or in an abandoned building. On one occasion we worshipped in an old building that had a parlor-size pump organ. I had enough music lessons to get by with, so played it for the church service. Today, I still vividly remember this setting when I hear the hymn "Holy, Holy, Holy! Lord God Almighty." It has such a special meaning to me. I can still picture myself there singing with the soldiers.

I always had to drive the chaplain wherever he needed or wanted to go. It seemed like we spent a lot of time just sightseeing. On my side of the jeep, I had the name Geraldine painted on it. Of course I didn't need a visual reminder of my sweetheart back home!

One day as we were driving around on a particular country road he saw a house with a radio aerial. He said he would like to have a radio so told me to go into these German civilians' home and take theirs. Even though he was an officer with a rank of captain, I told him I couldn't do it. I refused because I knew that this would be stealing. I couldn't believe it when, without hesitating he took off his chaplains' insignia, put on his army pistol and went into this stranger's house. He soon came out smiling and carrying a huge table model radio. He took it with him everywhere he went, apparently without any guilt. Many nights I could hear him with the radio turned on. I know this wasn't the norm for chaplains to act this way, but it still bothered me quite a bit.

War Ends in Europe, May 8, 1945

We were at the Czechoslovakian border when the war ended in Europe on May 8, 1945. Everyone was celebrating. I decided to join in and pointed my carbine in the air, pulled the trigger and nothing! Nothing happened at all! Evidently the firing pin had jammed. My thoughts were, *What if this had happened when I needed it to defend myself earlier?* Though I never was faced with that challenge, I still sometimes have nightmares awakening with a chill, then I thank the Lord for his protection.

Most of the fighting was over by now but a few isolated snipers were continuing so caution was needed everywhere.

In May we were issued new uniform jackets called the Eisenhower jacket, more commonly known as the Ike jacket, which continued to be used by our armed forces until 1956. They were shorter and more comfortable (prologue.blogs.archives.gov).

The following message of congratulations and farewell was received by us in July of 1945:

From: Supreme H.Q. Allied Expeditionary Forces.

To: Soldiers, Sailors and Airmen of the Allied Expeditionary Forces!

The task which we set ourselves is finished, and the time has come for me to relinquish Combined Command.

In the name of the United States and the British Commonwealth, I should like to convey gratitude.

At times, conditions have been hard and the tasks to be performed arduous. No praise is too high for the manner in which you have surmounted every obstacle.

I should like, also, to add my own personal word of thanks to each one of you for the part you have played, and the contribution you have made to our joint victory.

Now that you are about to pass to other spheres of activity, I say Good-bye to you and wish you Good luck and God-Speed.

Signed, D.D.E.

The Atomic Bombs drop on Japan, August 6, 1945

After the first successful experimental atomic bomb blast (July 16, 1945), the Allied leaders meeting at Potsdam decided to end the war quickly by atomic bombardment. After Japan rejected the allied ultimatum of unconditional surrender, a United States heavy bomber dropped an atomic bomb on Hiroshima, an important industrial and military center, on August 6, 1945, causing a hundred-sixty-thousand casualties and destroying more than half the city. Russia, following the Potsdam agreements, declared war on Japan two days later and sent its troops into Manchuria and Korea. The next day the United States Air Force dropped an atomic bomb on Nagasaki, an important industrial city and seaport, causing terrible casualties and destruction. The Japanese government sued for peace and accepted the allied terms of unconditional surrender. General MacArthur accepted the Japanese surrender onboard the *USS Missouri* on September 2, 1945.

Meritorious Award

The 107th Ordnance Medium Maintenance Company was awarded the Meritorious Unit Commendation from the 82nd Airborne Division for our contribution during the Ardennes battles during the period December 24, 1944-February 22, 1945. General Order Number 252; HQ, Ninth Army; awarded June 17, 1945.

As of December 12, 1944 the 107th Ordnance Medium Maintenance Company was assigned to the 320th Ordnance Battalion, 59th Ordnance Group, of the Ninth Army.

APO 230 was HQ, First Army. The location of APO 230 was Dueren, Germany, beginning March 21, 1945; Burg, Germany, beginning April 10, 1945: Weimar, Germany, beginning May 5, 1945.

APO 757 was HQ, Allied Expeditionary Force. The location of APO 757 was Frankfurt, Germany, beginning May 29, 1945.

Finally on May 23rd all censorship of mail was lifted. Even so in writing home it was still hard to describe the horrors of war.

I had not had any time off for a while so finally I was given a furlough. I chose to go to England on May 26. I went by truck to Verviers,

Belgium, then by train to Paris, then Etretat, LeHarve, and boarded a *Liberty* ship to England.

On the train to London I viewed all the sights. I happened to run across our former captain who was now a major. I was so excited to see him that I called him, "Captain," and then after hesitating for a second we both laughed. I stayed in the Red Cross facility while there. This furlough (vacation) was going too fast! I was also able to go to Bideford to visit my British friends, the Langdon family. They were glad to see me and to me it was the next best thing to being home.

After the furlough was finished I returned by the same route back to Germany. A strange thing happened though when we were based in the town of Weida, Germany. A few of us were billeted in a large house with lots of rooms being used by the headquarters unit. My bunk was on the second floor at the end of a hallway with enough room for two of us. One night I was awakened by my roommate who was making some strange jabbering noises. This continued for several nights. I think he was faking it but not enough to convince anyone that he was crazy. I am sure he thought he could do this so he could be sent back to the US

A New Assignment

It was shortly after returning from furlough in England for duty in Germany that I found I was being re-assigned to leave Germany and join a replacement company in Metz, France. My assignment was to work in the office to do what I had much experience with, that being in charge of payrolls, with typing and record-keeping.

This was disappointing news to say the least! I should have been sent home because I had accumulated enough service points but someone higher-up had decided I was needed to fill a critical need in another company. It seemed so unfair to keep me, for I felt I had done my share of duty. Evidently they wanted someone who had experience with getting the company records in shape. This assignment was with the 920th Ordnance Heavy Automotive Maintenance Company under Captain Bentley F. Stansbury. Instead of being with the 107th Ordnance Medium Maintenance Company, the one in which I spent the major part of the World War II, my discharge papers now identified me with this new company.

I was able to get the records cleared and payrolls accomplished right away. One day the first sergeant became ill so I decided I would do something different, like blowing my whistle to let the men know when it was time to eat. We certainly couldn't forget to do that! They came running thinking something was up. I don't remember much else occurring during those last days waiting to return to the US.

While in Metz I sadly heard about a friend, James Mitchell, from my home town, who had been killed in action and was buried in a military cemetery at Nancy. With a heavy heart I was able to visit his grave and take a photo of it to send to his widow, Pearl Collins Mitchell, back in St. Albans. Pearl was in my high school graduating class and greatly appreciated this gesture.

FRAITURE CHATEAU BELGIUM

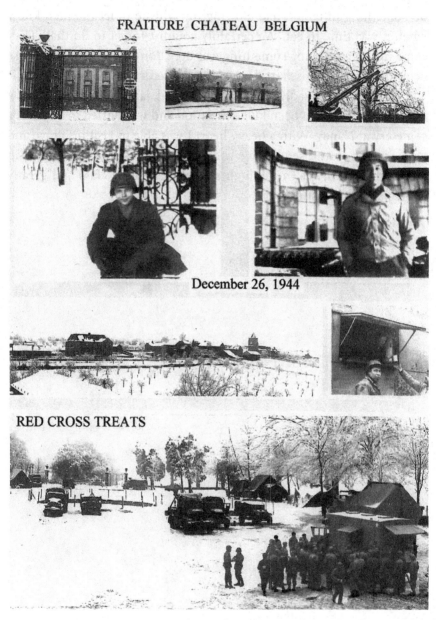

December 26, 1944

RED CROSS TREATS

(Photos by FT)

GERMONSTER CHATEAU - JANUARY 20, 1945

(Photos by FT)

VIELSALM BELGIUM JANUARY 28, 1945

MY OFFICE - Shattered Windows from Air Raid

Our Shop Repair Trucks ready for Tanks passing by.

(Street photos by FT)

Stolberg, Germany (Photo by FT)

Items found in a German factory

NOTRE DAME
Gothic architecture. It took over 180 years to complete, has 3 Organs (one which has 8,000 pipes). The circular stained-glass window displaying 84 panes of brilliantly colored glass; the Rose Window has a diameter of 42 feet.

PARIS

Church of Sacre Cour

June 13, 1945

Napoleons Tomb

(Photos by FT)

June 13, 1945

LaConcorde Square

P A R I S

Eifel Tower

LaMadalene Church

Champs Elyses

(Photos by FT)

Sgt. Forrest Thornton in 1945

A Belgium main street
(notice the public "restroom") in 1945 (Photo by FT)

St. Forrest Thornton in 1945

CAMP TOP HAT, BELGIUM Sept. 27, 1945

TROUP THEATER

Top: Sgt. Forrest Thornton in Verviers, Belgium,
in 1945 enjoying that first taste of ice cream;
Bottom: Camp Top Hat and homeward bound

Metz, France, and aqueduct while attached to the 920th Ord. Co. just before leaving on the train heading toward home.

Memorable train experience (Train photo by FT)

CHAPTER 9

Homeward Bound

One day as I casually went by the bulletin board to my extreme pleasure and surprise, I finally saw my name listed for return to the USA. How thrilled I was since I had been in the service four years and overseas for three long years! The day couldn't come soon enough!

The day came for me to leave as I finally received my orders. On September 8, 1945, I excitedly threw my duffle bag with all my belongings in the back of the truck. But when I stepped on the back bumper my foot slipped and I ended up spraining my ankle! Even though the pain was excruciating, I had to force myself to not let on for fear that I wouldn't get to go home. How ironic would that have been to have to stay after waiting so long for my discharge!

I went by truck to Reims, France, to a place called the halfway house. I found a medic who gave me a stretch band to wrap around my throbbing ankle. This bothered me off and on for several years. Since I had some time yet I went to Paris for a short visit with my friend, Sergeant Earl Daniel, and was able to go to church with him.

From there I travelled by train to Namur, Belgium, followed by Camp Top Hat in Antwerp, Belgium. What a train ride that was. The train was headed to Charleville near Namur, Belgium, where it stopped long enough for us to get some food. Since it was Sunday evening, the cook had the day off so all we got was cold baloney, cheese, crackers, fruit and coffee. The ancient coaches had been stripped of all the amenities such as windows and doors. The coach I was in felt and sounded like it had square wheels going thump, thump, thump. One of the doors had been put up on the luggage rack so I climbed up there and slept for the night. Again my army life had conditioned me to sleep in many places.

It was such a treat to be out of the war zone and have the freedom to enjoy an American camp with many things I had long forgotten such as: hot showers, clean clothes, hot food, free movies, and my favorite ice cream. Just to be able to move about without being in danger of being shot at was a real plus.

Most of our years in Europe we didn't have the luxury of showers very often.

The army special services set-up what they called a shower point that was in a tent out in the middle of a field near a stream. We would go in one end of the tent, take off everything to take a shower, get clean clothes and exit the other end feeling so much better than when we entered.

I found out that I would be traveling on the *Rensselear Victory Ship* leaving Antwerp on Oct. 4, 1945, with my shipment number being (RE-2019A-27). So I sent a cable home giving them this information.

We sailed by the White Cliffs of Dover, England about 6 pm. We were twenty-three-hundred miles from Boston on October 6, but three days later we were still a thousand-fifty miles from port. Fortunately the weather was pleasant all the way because it was a slow eight days. Finally, I glimpsed the sight of the US shoreline. This was the most welcomed vision! On arrival at port I was just forty-one days short of being gone overseas for three years.

Welcome Home and Wedding Bells

The ship docked in Boston Harbor on October 12, 1945. It is impossible to describe the feeling to be back home. That afternoon, as if in a dream, I walked down the gangplank and under the huge sign that said: "WELCOME HOME WELL DONE."

We boarded a bus staying overnight in Camp Miles Standish near Boston. It was so strange to me to be able to use a telephone or even to go into town without having to carry my rifle.

During all these four years away, Gerry was working at the telephone company and faithfully writing and waiting for me to return. She had been at home one evening listening to the radio when she heard the broadcaster announce ship arrivals. She just couldn't believe it when they said the *Rensselear Victory Ship* had arrived at Boston. I called home that evening but struggling for words, I found myself not knowing what to say. I was overcome with the enormity of it all. But I let everyone know that I had arrived safely and quickly ended my call.

The next day we were sent by train to Fort Meade, Maryland. Then by morning the train headed west by New River arriving at Charleston, West Virginia, that evening where we stopped to refuel. Some of the soldiers quickly ran to the telephones at the station. I knew I might miss getting back on board before the train left so I decided not to chance it. We continued on, passing through my hometown of St. Albans about midnight on October 15th. At this point I had gone to the back of the train to the platform. Just as we were to pass near the St. Albans train depot, I saw Geraldine waiting to cross the tracks after getting off work on her way to spend the night with her aunt Emma Wood! I waived to her and yelled but with the noise and smoke from the train she didn't see or hear me. It was also pretty dark outside but just that glimpse was all it took to make me more anxious to get home! Too bad I couldn't have hopped off then and there, but we had to continue on for our final discharge.

The train was picking up speed so it could cross over the very steep Coal Mountain and then on to Fort Knox, Kentucky. There I was honorably discharged from the US Army on October 19, 1945. I didn't realize at that time that I would need some clothes for returning to civilian life. I should have insisted on seeing a supply sergeant and asking for some replacements, which I really needed. So I ended up being stuck wearing my uniform for a while.

Several of us were heading east from Ft. Knox so we found and chartered a bus to Huntington, West Virginia. I called my mother and dad asking them to meet me late that evening. What a welcome sight at the bus station that night to be met by Gerry along with my dad and mom. It was an exciting time for sure! We arrived home late then I turned around and drove Gerry on to her mother's home. I was still floating on air so it didn't register in my mind that soon we would be married.

Wedding Day 1945

It was so good to see everyone after being gone for that length of time. The next morning Gerry and I went to the Kanawha County courthouse in Charleston to get our marriage license. I was so anxious I couldn't believe we had to wait three days for the wedding. But I told myself what was three days compared to the four years we had waited! We came back to St. Albans and stopped at the pastor's house to ask if he would marry us, to which he replied yes. Then the next day we went to church together.

Mom had already made the dresses for the girls. Gerry had bought the veil and borrowed her cousin's gown. The rehearsal was Monday evening and, at last, we were married on Tuesday evening, October 23, 1945, in the First Baptist Church of St. Albans, West Virginia.

Reception

We had a lovely reception at Gerry's grandmother's home and we spent our honeymoon in Virginia. Now as I look back on those days of war I realize that had I not had a personal faith in God's Son, Jesus, who never once failed me, I would have had a tougher time coping than I did. There was the hope that I really would be returning home to marry my lovely lady. Then we could continue with our dreams of life together as we had planned prior to this interlude of four long, long years waiting, waiting, waiting, and finally coming home to that nice welcome, and then the wedding, and our wonderful honeymoon.

OCT. 3 BOARDING SHIP SS-RENSSELEAR VICTORY

TROOP ASSIGNMENT CARD

Compartment No. 3 B — Bunk No.

Each man upon finding his bunk will place his
equipment and himself thereon until released by his
Ship's Company Commander.

NO SMOKING in Troop Quarters At Any Time.

This card will be used as a meal ticket throughout the voyage.   SAVE IT!   DON'T LOSE IT!

SAILED OCT. 4 - 4pm from ANTWERP Harbor   23 FREE MEALS

LOUNGING ON DECK

COUNTING THE DAYS

BOSTON HARBOR   OCTOBER 12, 1945

EXCITEMENT - SEARCHING FOR LAND

HOME - AT LAST

WELCOME HOME   WELL DONE

OCT. 12, 1945

Wow! -Would you look at my new Bride!
(October 23, 1945)

CHAPTER 10

Life after the War

I did not go back to work at the bank after the war ended nor did I go to work for my dad at the store. My grandfather was still working there and said he really didn't have an opening for a full-time extra employee. Instead, I was offered a job at Union Carbide Chemical Company in South Charleston, February of 1946. I started there as a clerk in the drafting room of the engineering department. Along with working I was also studying engineering by correspondence. It wasn't long until I was promoted to a drafting position where my first assignment was drawing a plot plan of the Texas City Plant in Texas. I learned to do pipe drafting then later learned how to make lists of materials to build a chemical plant.

I was later promoted as a group leader with five men working with me. Around 1963 I was moved into the design engineering group and given a title as project group assistant. All these jobs were not something I asked for; they were the Lord's doing. Many times during my working days I saw the Lord's hand in these events.

Move to Texas

In 1966, I had a choice to consider a move to the engineering office in Houston. After much prayer and weighing all the options, I decided it was the Lord's leading, so we packed up in August and moved to Texas. The Houston office was very different and was managed under the international branch of Union Carbide. Being in a big city was a huge change from my small town back in West Virginia.

The move was quite an adjustment for me and my family. In fact our first Thanksgiving in our new house stands out as a vivid memory. Previous Thanksgivings had always been a huge family affair at my wife's grandmother's house up on the hill. Probably thirty or forty people would be there at a time with so much food along with lots of laughter and love. But now we knew no one in Houston plus had no relatives living nearby. On top of that, I was tied up with jury duty all week so Gerry wasn't able to shop for the ingredients she would need to make a Thanksgiving dinner. In those days we only had one car plus the stores weren't open at night for her to shop when I got back. The trial lasted until late Wednesday evening. Of course getting home that late didn't leave us any option but to go to a corner convenient store and try to get something that would somewhat resemble a meal. It certainly wasn't what we were used to plus didn't include turkey!

In a few years I was given a new title of engineering technician. This title stuck with me until I retired. One of my jobs was to check all the new work to make sure it met all the engineering standards. It had some challenges but was very interesting.

Early Retirement?

January 1972 the Houston office was being cut back from three-hundred people to about twenty. I had completed twenty-six years with Carbide and was then offered a choice between three options. It looked like the best one was to take a special early retirement offered to those over age fifty. Well, this was a big decision to make, one that could have tremendous consequences.

We knew the Lord had definitely led us in our move to Houston. Did this mean that we should return to West Virginia? While the job situations in West Virginia were very bleak, the Houston job market was much alive. After much prayer and a peace from the Lord, I chose to take the early retirement and I began the search for another job here in Houston. The early retirement pay was only enough to meet the monthly house payments.

I immediately prepared my resume and sent it out to all the major engineering companies, many with which I had personal contact.

Texaco and My Best Work Years

After several interviews I was hired by Texaco. I took a week's vacation then began my new job afterwards. My new assignment was in the engineering standards group. This became the best job I ever had and the final few years of work were very good years. I became a valve specialist where I was in touch with all the major valve companies around the globe. My job was to choose appropriate valves for refinery use, those that met the standards that Texaco wanted. I traveled to some of the manufacturing plants for inspections and approvals then also went to refineries to help when they had valve problems.

I knew I would have to continue working past my sixty-fifth birthday since Tim, my son, was still in college. But before that time arrived I was given a special retirement package and retired the end of September, 1985.

A Final Retirement

My boss, Ed Bane, gave me a very special retirement luncheon in the dining room of a department store in downtown, Houston. He gave me a certificate and a bronze plaque commemorating my fourteen years of service to the company.

By the way, at age ninety-six, I'm still working part time here in Houston, Texas. Though the pay isn't the same the rewards are greater. I'm especially delighted that I do not have to get up so early now.

I've had the privilege of teaching seniors computer classes. That was the career I chose when I turned eighty! I was a charter member instructor teaching beginner's computer classes for almost six years (2000-2005) at the Jim and JoAnn Fonteno Senior Education Center, Houston, Texas. Hundreds were waiting to take the class but I could only take eight at a time. I've also enjoyed oil painting over the years but here lately have been working on genealogies and also these memoires.

I am very thankful for those forty years of continuous employment. It was only because of the Lord's faithfulness that I had any success at all. I trusted in the Lord to guide me in each endeavor and He never failed me. Who would ever have thought or dreamed that a West Virginia hillbilly such as I could ever live anywhere but in the mountains? Where I lived, the norm was to be born and die in the same location.

WWII Veteran Forrest Thornton

EPILOGUE:
A HEART OF THANKS

I am certainly glad at my age of ninety-six to be able to recall happenings of events that occurred in those years away from familiar surroundings. With maturity comes a sense of better judgment and appreciation. If I could do it over again I would try to learn from others and try to improve and/or excel. I have greater respect for those who knew better or seemed to make better choices.

I also would like to have gained a grade higher rank than sergeant; staff sergeant would be fine. I knew that I could not qualify for any officer level but respected those who were the officers of the 107th Ordnance Medium Maintenance Company.

Some of the experiences spent in service during the war didn't seem important at the time. I was only thinking of getting away from the office and camp duties to explore and enjoy cities, towns and the country.

Church services were always important for me. At church I always found new friends and I benefited from the words spoken from the pastor. Although the language differences and church services varied, handshakes were always welcome. Once I found a quaint, little church in Belgium and went there on a Sunday finding that they had communion served after the message was over. I couldn't understand some of the language except a few words like God, Jesus, or Bible. The communion was served by the pastor or an elder where he had a bronze container with wine or grape juice in it. He carried a towel to wipe the brim after each person partook. Being in the presence with like-minded people was always a joy for me.

Thinking back to the end of WWII, things were very peaceful compared to the world situation now. In this year of 2016 the news is very alarming. It looks like war will occur again as many nations are threatening to start another large scale conflict. We need today to recommit ourselves to the only one who can give us peace in our hearts. And that person is Jesus Christ.

My Camera and I

My camera that I used all during the war was a folding model of Kodak that I usually carried with me when I was out and around. I always kept my camera on a strap or in my shirt pocket. All the Officers of the 107th knew I had a camera so many requested copies of any photos I had made of them.

Interesting Memory

We crossed the English Channel in late August of 1944 when heading toward the beaches of Normandy, and a huge storm was brewing. The liberty ship I was in, *The SS James Caldwell*, lifted anchor to proceed south. The storm was so bad we had to lay anchor not too far from the White Cliffs of Dover, England. I recalled a popular song during those days by Vera Lynn titled, "There'll be Blue Birds over the White Cliffs of Dover." I thought of just a few phrases like, "Blue birds over the Cliffs of Dover tomorrow, just wait and see...when the world is free...' Of course I didn't see any blue birds until later years but did see the world being set *free*. Thank you *Lord!*

Axis Sally

I didn't have a radio while overseas but I read about a person named Sally in the military newspapers during WWII, which explained her program and false claims.

Axis Sally had a radio program from Berlin all during WWII. Ironically, her broadcast was called the Home Sweet Home Hour, but it was a propaganda program intended to create homesickness among American GIs. She was said to often make references to the unfaithfulness of wives and girlfriends back home in an effort to demoralize the troops. Her broadcast consisted of American songs, words of defeatism, anti-Jewish propaganda, and harsh criticisms of FDR. It stopped just two days before the German surrender of May 6, 1945.

Of course, there were occasions for me to hear my own favorite patriotic songs, or at least to whistle them or recite them in my mind. It was important for all of us to keep thinking about those things that would give us hope, courage, and inspiration. (See Appendix D.)

Victory Parade

Throughout all the years since the end of WWII, I did not have an opportunity to be in a victory parade until May 25, 1991. Houston had a special welcome parade for the Desert Storm troops. I read in the newspaper that all veterans of any war were welcome to take part in the parade so I decided, *why not?* Gerry, our daughter Marilyn, and I went and we enjoyed the parade immensely. I found my old army hat, which is all I have left of my uniform. I put on a tan shirt and trousers; pinned on my service ribbons and away we went. Arriving downtown I was pleasantly surprised to see an old half-track vehicle available for me along with other veterans to ride on. I stood by the anti-aircraft gun, which was on the back, and waved to everyone along the route of the parade. As the parade started, the Channel 13 camera crew boarded the half-track and Mr. Alan Hemberger, one of their newscasters, interviewed me. This was shown on the evening news.

June 4, 1994, I was in a parade marking D-Day, 50 years prior, in downtown Houston, and that was also thrilling.

A Later Special Event

On April 8, 2010, I received a surprise package by mail. It contained new service medals from Congressman John Culberson. Some of these medals I didn't even know I had earned during World War II. The photo of my medals is on the back cover of this book. The following letter accompanied the package:

> US House of Representatives
> Letter from John Culberson
> 7th District, Texas
> Dear Mr. Thornton,
>
> In response to my inquiry on your behalf, the National Personnel Record Center has provided the

medals which you had been awarded but not received for your service in the United States Army.

I would like to thank you for your bravery in defending our country. You served with honor, dignity, and courage, setting aside your own impulses to ensure that our flag represents the strongest virtues that God endowed in humanity.

Although God grants us the rights of life, liberty and the pursuit of happiness, we are dependent on our soldiers to protect and defend those rights.

Thank you for your service to our great nation and God bless you and your family.

Sincerely, John Culberson, Member of Congress

Our Freedom!

We are, "One nation under God! With liberty and justice for all."

I served in WWII for four long years and many lonely times while protecting our liberties, including our freedom *of* worship-religion and not freedom *from* worship-religion. Today our country has turned away from Christianity, not allowing schools or students to respect our Christian faith.

As individual citizens of the US, we do have freedom of speech, press, *religion* and petition. "Congress shall make no law respecting an establishment of religion, or prohibiting the free exercise thereof; or abridging the freedom of speech, or of the press; or the right of the people peaceably to assemble, and to petition the government for a redress of grievances" (Bill of Rights).

It is my hope and prayer that in some small way, my thoughts, reflections, and shared information may bring encouragement, hope, solace, and a renewed commitment to faith in our country and in our God.

Christ is the Victory that overcomes the world!

2ND CORP

9TH ARMY

1ST ARMY

7TH CORP

SERVICE OF SUPPLY U.S.A

3 YRS - OVERSEAS

SERVICE OF SUPPLY EUROPEAN THEATRE

My Service Patches

APPENDIX A

Service Medals

My Army service medals (pictured on the back cover) include:

1. The American Defense Service Medal, a military award of the United States Armed Forces established on June 28, 1941. It was for active duty between September 8, 1939 and December 7, 1941 and the colors were yellow blue, red and white.

2. The European Theater Medal, a military award of the United States Armed Forces first created on November 6, 1942 with the colors being brown, green, white and red.

   For each of these battles I was authorized to wear a miniature bronze star which was attached to the European Theater of operation. Each star represented the four battles I fought in over a period of ten months. Our 107th Ordnance Company was with the 83rd Ordnance Battalion during this time:

   Northern France (July 25 1944 to Sept. 14 1944)
   Rhineland (Sept. 15 1944 to Mar. 21 1945)
   Ardennes-Alsace (Dec. 16 1944 to Jan 25 1945)
   Central Europe (Mar 22 1945 to May 11 1945)

3. The Army Good Conduct Medal, established on Aug. 26 1940 for enlisted men of the Army with the color being red with three white stripes on each side.

4. The World War II Victory Medal, a service medal of the United States Military established on 6 July 1945 with the colors being blue, green, orange, red and white.

5. The American Campaign Medal, a military award of the United States Armed Forces for military service in the American Theater of Operations during World War II. A similar medal, known as the American Defense Service Medal was awarded for active duty service prior to the United States entry into World War II. The colors are blue, white, black and red.

APPENDIX B

Service Timeline

Forrest Thornton's Dates of Service during WW 2

Nov 21 1941 – USA Inducted US Army
Nov 30 1942 – England
Sept 4 1944 – France
Oct 15 1944 – Belgium
Nov 16 1944 – Holland
Dec 25 1944 – Belgium
Feb 20 1045 – Germany
Jun 12 1945 – France
Sept 26 1945 – Belgium
Oct 12 1945 – USA
Oct 19 1045 – Honorable Discharge

Forrest Thornton's Military Career
July 1 1941 – Notice of Classification
November 1, 1941 – Selected for training and service as Private
July 11, 1942 – Promoted to Corporal Technician 5th grade, as the company clerk
July 5, 1943 – Promoted to Sgt. Technician 4th grade
Oct 19 1945 – Honorable Discharge

Amazing Family Parallels

Great Grandfather Addison Henry Thornton

Reflecting on my life and participation in the war, I am struck to consider some similarities of events between my Great Grandfather Addison Henry Thornton and me:

ADDISON	FORREST born 80 yrs. later
--- Both of us with -- 5 ft. 7 in height -- brown hair -- Blue eyes.	
July 13, 1840 **Born**	Feb. 2, 19**20**
Jun. 15, 18**61** Enlisted in CSA -	Nov. 21, 19**41** -Drafted into US Army
Sept. 1, 1865 Promoted **to Sgt.**	July 5, 1943 promoted **to Sgt.**
April to Jun 1865 - POW 3 Mos.	------------------------------------
------------------------------------	Foreign Service - 1942 to 1945
June 20, 18**65 4 yrs.** discharged	Oct. 19, 1945 **term 4 yrs.**
Oct. 17 18**65 age 25 Married**	Oct. 23, 1945 **age 25**
Both Wives Two Yrs. younger	
Apr.16, 1867 **First Child born**	Aug 2, 1947
1868 - VA to WV **Major Move**	**1966 - WV to TX**
Three more children	Three more children

===

A Timeline: Civil War, World War One, and World War Two

Civil War – Great Grandfather- Addison Henry Thornton (b.1840-d.1919)
World War I – Uncle Lewis Madison Bird (b.1896-d.1960)
World War II – Forrest Ardin Thornton (b.1920-)

- Sgt. Addison Henry Thornton – 1861 to 1865
  Enlisted - June 15, 1861, 57th Virginia Infantry,
  Discharged - June 20, 1865.

The American Civil War began on Friday, April 12, 1861 and ended on Tuesday, May 9, 1865. At that time, Abraham Lincoln was the 16th president in 1861. On April 12, 1861, America was divided into two parts. The North was the United States of America. The South was the Confederate States of America. The president of the Confederate States of America was Jefferson Davis. The president of the United States of America was Abraham Lincoln. They were considered the presidents of the Civil War.

- Pvt. Lewis Madison Bird was drafted in 1918 and served in Co. E, 306th Infantry during World War I in France.

My Uncle Lewis Madison Bird was born April 7, 1896 Browns Creek, Putnam Co., WV and died Mar. 9, 1960 in St. Albans, Kanawha Co., WV.
He never talked very much about what he did while in service. But I remember that he never liked being away from home. This was known

as the war to end all wars. It began on 28 July 1914 and lasted until 11 November 1918 in Europe. Woodrow Wilson was US President.

- Sgt. Forrest A. Thornton – 1941 to 1945 - World War II.

I was inducted into the US Army and assigned into the ordnance branch of service with the 107th Ordnance Medium Maintenance Company. My assignment was as the company clerk, preparing payrolls as well as performing other military duties.

President Franklin Roosevelt signed the Declaration of War against Japan in December 1941 shortly after the attack on Pearl Harbor. He remained president for the duration of war until his death in office in April of 1945, less than a month before the surrender of Germany. President Harry Truman succeeded him and saw the end of the war under his administration. World War II is called the deadliest conflict in human history.

During the Paris Peace conference of 1919, Britain, France, the United States and Italy imposed their terms in a series of treaties. The League of Nations was formed with the aim of preventing any repetition of such a conflict. This, however, failed with weakened states, economic depression, renewed European nationalism, and the German feeling of humiliation contributing to the rise of Nazism, These conditions eventually contributed to WWII.

APPENDIX D

My Favorite Scripture Verses

"For God so loved the world that he gave his one and only Son, that whoever believes in him [Jesus] shall not perish but have eternal life" (John 3:16, NIV).

"Surely goodness and love will follow me all the days of my life, and I will dwell in the house of the Lord forever (Psalms 23:6, NIV).

"Praise be to the name of God for ever and ever; wisdom and power are his. He changes times and seasons; he deposes kings and raises up others. He gives wisdom to the wise and knowledge to the discerning. He reveals deep and hidden things; he knows what lies in darkness, and light dwells with him" (Daniel 2:20-22, NIV).

"If we claim to be without sin, we deceive ourselves and the truth is not in us. If we confess our sins, he is faithful and just and will forgive us our sins and purify us from all unrighteousness" (1 John 1:8-9, NIV).

"Keep your servant also from willful sins; may they not rule over me. Then I will be blameless, innocent of great transgression. May these words of my mouth and this meditation of my heart be pleasing in your sight, Lord, my Rock and my Redeemer" (Psalm 19:13-14, NIV).

"Remember, Lord, your great mercy and love, for they are from of old. Do not remember the sins of my youth and my rebellious ways" (Psalm 25:6-7, NIV).

"I am the gate; whoever enters through me will be saved.[a] They will come in and go out, and find pasture. The thief comes only to steal and kill and destroy; I have come that they may have life, and have it to the full" (John 10:9-11, NIV).

"Surely goodness and love will follow me all the days of my life; and I will dwell in the house of the Lord forever" (Psalm 23:6, NIV).

My Favorite Anthems and Pledge

The following patriotic anthems always give me some thrills as I hear them. The first, *God Bless America* was written by Irving Berlin as a new patriotic song to mark the twentieth anniversary of the Armistice that ended World War I.

> While the storm clouds gather far across the sea
> Let us swear allegiance to a land that's free
> Let us all be grateful for a land so fair
> As we raise our voices in a solemn prayer
> God bless America, land that I love
> Stand behind her and guide her
> Through the night with a light from above
> From the mountains, to the prairies
> To the oceans white with foam
> God bless America
> My home sweet home

I especially love the line, "From the mountains, to the prairies to the oceans white with foam - God bless America, My home sweet home"

My other favorite is, *America! America,* with the lines:

> God shed His grace on thee
> And crown thy good with brotherhood
> From sea to shining sea!

My Pledge Affirmed

I end my thoughts with the affirmation of my allegiance:
"I pledge allegiance to the Flag
of the United States of America,
and to the Republic for which it stands:
one Nation under God, indivisible,
With Liberty and Justice for all."

BIBLIOGRAPHY

Charleston Daily Mail. "The Japanese Navy Attack at Pearl Harbor, Hawaii," [Charleston, WV] 12 Dec. 1994. Print.

"FDR Congress/WW2." Words and Deeds in American History. Library of Congress. Online. Internet. Retrieved 2015. Web. [https://memory.loc.gov/ammem/mcchtml/corhome.html].

"FDR Programs." *Wikipedia: The Free Encyclopedia.* Wikimedia Foundation, Inc. Online. Internet. Retrieved 2015. Web.

Hauck, Gary L. *Exploring Humanities Around the World.* Bloomington, IN: iUniverse, 2008.

Holy Bible, New International Version®, NIV® Copyright ©1973, 1978, 1984, 2011 by Biblica, Inc. (Formerly, International Bible Society). Web.

Houston Chronicle, "D-Day," [Houston, TX] 3 Apr. 1944. Print.

"Ike Jacket." Prologue.blogs.archives.gov. Retrieved 2015. Web.

"Patriotic Songs and National Anthems." *Wikipedia: The Free Encyclopedia.* Wikimedia Foundation, Inc. Online. Internet. Retrieved 2015. Web.

Pettus, Louise. "The Carolina Maneuvers." Rootsweb. Online. Internet. Retrieved 2015. Web.

"Red Ball Express." Online. Internet. Retrieved 2015. Web. [transchool.lee.army.mil/museum/transportation%20museum/redballintro.htm].

Sulzberger, C.L., and Abrose, S. "Adolf Hitler's Death." *American Heritage New History of World War II.* New York: Viking, 1997. Print.

"Utah Beach." Army.Mil Features. Online. Internet. Retrieved 2015. Web. [http://www.army.mil/d-day/index.html].

"V1 Flying Bomb." Army.Mil Features. Online. Internet. Retrieved 2015. Web. [http://www.army.mil/d-day/index.html].

"WV Battleship." Words and Deeds in American History. Library of Congress. Online. Internet. Retrieved 2015. Web. [https://memory. loc.gov/ammem/mcchtml/corhome.html], [www.lostimagesofww2. com/photos/places/louisiana-maneuvers.php\l].

Printed in the United States
By Bookmasters